"Whether you desire to build a coaching business, or whether you've become an accidental coach as I have, Brenda Chand's *You Can Coach* will be invaluable in helping you more effectively help others become their best. It is chock-full of practical details, I would have gone further faster as a coach if I'd had this volume a few years ago! The discussion of the mindset/attitude needed to be an effective coach is, by itself, worth the price of this book. If you are helping or want to help others, this book will help you."

—CAROL TANKSLEY, MD, DMin, Author, Speaker, Personal Coach, President Dr. Carol Ministries

"Dr. Brenda Chand is a lifelong student and professor of coaching and leadership! In this volume, she showcases her wisdom in an encyclopedia on coaching. Brenda, a practitioner of coaching, rightly divides the history, clarifies with definitions, and categorizes this arena of life. This must-read is a great work representing a lot of valuable research! Well done!"

—DR. GARNET PIKE, President & Cofounder, SpiritLife Ministries

"Dr. Brenda Chand's Dream Releaser Training has produced some of the top coaches I have seen in the last twenty years. This book identifies the DNA of why that consistently happens. Written with clarity and brevity, it is a substantial addition to both your pre- and post-coach training essential library. In fact, it covers the territory of four books in one! I highly recommend her expertise, perspective, staff insights, and content of all that she offers. Most importantly, your own story and heart for coaching others will be wonderfully expanded."

—DR. JOSEPH UMIDI, EVP Regent University

"Dr. Brenda Chand synthesizes the concepts of biblical discipleship and corporate mentoring as she joins you on your journey to success—not as a sideline cheerleader but as a player-coach in the game of life, affirming the truth that you are a winner! She is your playbook!"

—KENNETH ULMER, PhD, DMin, Trustee, The King's University

"Throughout the many years that I have known Brenda, one thing stands out to me: she continually invests in her personal and professional growth. Her example is of utmost importance if we want to offer relevant and substantial training to others. Her intuitive nature enables her to approach coaching with the expertise of making heart connections, which are necessary to encourage growth in those we lead. Brenda has spent years training coaches—not just individuals—thus her methodology is proven, and her wisdom is sound. I'm grateful to benefit from her insight as I know you will be also as you absorb and apply all that she has generously given us here. I cannot wait to have this book in my hands as I know that I will benefit greatly from it!"

—COLLEEN ROUSE, Pastor, Author, and
Founder & Director of Thrive Today

"Sometimes the hardest part of achieving your goals is getting started. I'm here to recommend you start here with Brenda Chand's *You Can Coach*. When it comes to meeting fitness goals, the hardest lift is often the lift off the couch. The same goes for making lifestyle changes, creating new habits, healing from past hurts, starting a business, or meeting career goals. Getting started and staying committed is where accountability becomes necessary. We need community, and we need expert coaching. Chand's approach in *You Can Coach* teaches us everything we need and want to know about coaching. Her insights show us why coaching changes lives, how to coach and be coached, and how to become a certified coach and trainer. Get started, be a sponge, and learn everything you can, so you can keep moving forward."

—LISA KAI, Pastor of Inspire Church, Author, *Perfectly You*

"If you want to maximize your personal and professional potential, this book is for you! I am fortunate enough to be a Dream Releaser Coaching (DRC) graduate. Before I entered this process, I was stuck both in my personal and professional life, and unbeknownst to me, the hardest battle of my life was just before me when I enrolled in DRC. The curriculum included in this book literally saved my life! It gave me hope and energized me to walk through an unexpected illness. The insights and encouragement got me back on my feet again. You can get the same training (in the form of this book) at a bargain. The skills that I learned in DRC include the ability to coach my clients through using powerful questions that have brought clarity to the client-discovery process and multiplied my income. I unequivocally recommend this for coaches and entrepreneurs alike."

—MOREN ADENUBI, CCIM, CIPS, CPM, Managing Broker, Crown Realty Experts, Real Estate Instructor & Master Coach

Cover design by: Sara Young
Cover Photo by: Andrew van Tilborgh

ISBN: 978-1-954089-71-6   1 2 3 4 5 6 7 8 9 10

Printed in the United States of America

YOU

A PRACTICAL
GUIDE TO COACHING IN
EVERYDAY LIFE

CAN
COACH

BRENDA C. CHAND

INSPIRE

CONTENTS

Introduction 9

PART 1. THE BASICS OF COACHING 11

CHAPTER 1. What is Coaching? 13

CHAPTER 2. The History of Coaching 23

CHAPTER 3. Why People Want a Coach 27

CHAPTER 4. Proven Models 33

CHAPTER 5. Limitations 39

CHAPTER 6. Your Heart, Your Future 45

PART 2. THE PURPOSE OF COACHING 59

CHAPTER 7. Unlocking Goals and Dreams 61

CHAPTER 8. Building Hope 71

CHAPTER 9. Forward-Focused Coaching 79

CHAPTER 10. Facilitating Change 87

CHAPTER 11. Stages of Change 91

PART 3. THE PRACTICE OF COACHING 103

CHAPTER 12. The Importance of Self-Discovery 105

CHAPTER 13. Active Listening 109

CHAPTER 14. Motivational Interviewing 115

CHAPTER 15. Using PLANS 121

CHAPTER 16. Setting SMART Goals 127

CHAPTER 17. The Grow Model 139

CHAPTER 18. Overcoming Barriers 143

CHAPTER 19. Focus on Core Values 151

CHAPTER 20. The Elusive "Balanced Life" 157

CHAPTER 21. Establishing Your Mission,
                Vision, and Purpose 171
CHAPTER 22. Becoming a Change Agent 187

PART 4. COMMON TOPICS IN COACHING 191
CHAPTER 23. Instilling Self-Confidence 193
CHAPTER 24. Resolving Conflict 201
CHAPTER 25. Financial Freedom 217
CHAPTER 26. Charting a Career Trajectory 227
CHAPTER 27. Leading Through Chaos 237
CHAPTER 28. Personal Development 251
CHAPTER 29. Weight Control 261
CHAPTER 30. Transcultural Coaching 269

PART 5. COACHING AS A BUSINESS 277
CHAPTER 31. Choosing Your Niche 279
CHAPTER 32. Organizing Your Business 293
CHAPTER 33. Acquiring Clients 303

Acknowledgments 313
About the Author: Brenda C. Chand 315
About the Dream Releaser Coaching Program 317
Resources 325
Additional Reading 327

INTRODUCTION

S tepping into the lives of people and helping them take steps forward in their relationships and careers is one of the most fulfilling roles anyone can play. That's what coaches do. In the last two decades, I've had the privilege to train hundreds of professional coaches. Each one began with a spark of hope that connecting with a coach could change their lives, and as they saw progress, they saw themselves assuming that pivotal role in the lives of others.

You've picked up this book because you have a heart for people. You want to see them grow, overcome difficulties, make a difference, and fulfill their dreams. Your friends probably already come to you for advice when they feel stuck and comfort when they're struggling. You want to be more skilled and more effective as you talk with these friends . . . and you may be wondering if becoming a professional coach is the right path for you.

This is a companion book to the *Professional Coaching Handbook*. The handbook is designed for those who have already answered the call to become coaches, and it gives them additional insights, principles, and skills. The book you hold in your hands is more of an introduction to coaching—but it's still packed with plenty of valuable content.

We can't give someone resources and wisdom we don't possess, so it's important to be coached before you become a coach and as you coach others—to be a sponge to absorb all the life principles you can hold so that when others squeeze you, those principles flow out into their lives and situations. So, as you read this book, find a coach, a mentor, or a gifted friend to walk through it with you to answer your questions, correct any misguided thinking (which we all have), and point you in a direction that leads to effectiveness and fulfillment.

I've enjoyed many moments in my relationships with coaches, and I never tire of seeing the joy on their faces and hearing the excitement in their voices when they tell me how they've helped people find new sources of hope, overcome obstacles, and experience more fulfillment than they ever dreamed was possible.

In some chapters in this book, I'll assume you're primarily interested in helping your friends, but a number of chapters address the principles and skills necessary for professional coaches. You'll find a few case studies inserted throughout the book to help you apply the principles in the chapters.

I've asked some of our finest Dream Releaser Coaching trainers to write about their experiences and suggestions for those who are entering the field of coaching. You'll see their contributions in various chapters.

You may want to begin in chapter 1 and read right through to chapter 33, or you may have particular questions and look for the chapters that give the answers you're looking for. There's no right or wrong way to use this book. However you choose to read it, I trust it will encourage you, challenge you, and give you handles on how to step into the lives of others to help them take steps forward.

Brenda C. Chand

Brenda C. Chand

PART 1

The Basics of Coaching

CHAPTER 1

WHAT IS COACHING?

CASE STUDY

Barbara had been in a longtime state of frustration and knew that she needed a real change if she was going to remain effective in her career. She had been working in a globally recognized corporation for twelve years and held the title of Executive Coordinator in an engineering group. Her responsibilities included facilitating weekly staff meetings with nine engineers, and keeping them on task to meet crucial deadlines. As much as she appreciated her job, it became apparent that her position and outgoing personality incorrectly advertised her as the resident problem solver. It wasn't uncommon for coworkers to stop by her office several times a day with issues and questions—expecting advice, if not the actual solution. Instead of putting her professional foot forward, she fell into the trap of taking on false responsibility. She didn't know how to empower others to pursue their own results, and this led to her becoming disgruntled and frustrated. It affected every aspect of her life. It was part of her job description to be supportive—not to complete their tasks.

Her boss was one of the corporation's vice presidents, and the two of them had a very open relationship. He took note of her growing discontentment and suggested that she investigate to discover her passion and purpose in life and then go for it. Her position wasn't in jeopardy, but she sensed her effectiveness had become marginal. Acting on her boss's encouragement, she entered life coach training. Her paradigm of problem solving and assisting others was immediately shifted. Barbara experienced an "aha" moment from the outset of her training and devoured the coaching material, readily embracing key coaching concepts. It was as if someone had breathed instruction into her life and set her on a completely new path. She began applying the core principles she was taught, and her way of maneuvering progress during the weekly meetings was noticed instantly. Rather than providing solutions, she presented an open forum for discussion that allowed the engineers to brainstorm into success with each project. Her attitude changed to one of optimism because she no longer felt bogged down with the responsibility she had previously adopted as her daily work style. She brought optimism to the table, and encouraged team members to dream bigger and strategize smarter.

After only a short time, her boss called her into his office to applaud her on the changes she had made. They talked about the success of her finding her own personal purpose and how it was affecting everything about her. He began to really value her opinion and on several occasions brought scenarios into her office and asked her to coach him through the decision-making process. Her boss respected the advantage that life coaching had brought into her life and how it could personally impact him in a great way.

Later, Barbara's boss was offered a position of Senior Vice President, which required him to serve one year outside of the US. Before he was transferred to South Africa, he explored the benefits of going through coach training himself because he saw the value it could bring to his new position.

Coaching provided the avenue needed for Barbara to make a complete life shift. She learned to no longer offer solutions and advice, but rather to provide time, space, and an environment of listening that allows others to conceive their own hope, abilities, and dreams. She has now gained great satisfaction from empowering others to discover their own potential and equipping leaders to forge ahead into success.

At its most basic level, coaching is simply caring enough to step into another person's life to offer the wisdom and insights we've learned. In this way, all of us who express empathy and support serve as coaches. But in recent decades, the concept has become formalized with training and certification to assure professional excellence. All coaches, no matter how skilled and experienced, are in the process of learning and growing so they can become more effective in helping others.

There are a number of ways to define coaching. Some of them include:

- The International Coaching Federation (ICF) defines coaching as "partnering with clients in a thought-provoking and creative process that inspires them to maximize their personal and professional potential."[1]

---

1 https://coachingfederation.org/about.

- In *Christian Coaching: Helping Others Turn Potential into Reality*, Gary Collins's definition of coaching is "the art and practice of working with a person or group in the process of moving from where they are to where God wants them to be."[2]

- Coaching helps people who want to "get unstuck, build their confidence, expand their vision for the future, fulfill their dreams, unlock their potential, increase their skills, move through transitions, and take practical steps toward their goals."[3]

- Coaching is moving a person from the place in which they are—through active listening, asking powerful questions, identifying their goals, providing encouragement, and holding them accountable—to reach their destiny for life.

The greatest explorer on this earth never takes voyages as long as those of the man who descends to the depth of his heart.

—JULIEN GREEN

- Coaches are professionals who are not necessarily therapists. Typically, a coach is trained in the skills required to move an individual through the change processes and stages and/or is an expert with a proven track record of success in a given area.

- According to Sir John Whitmore, one of the great strengths of coaching is that it "requires expertise in coaching but not in the

---

2 Gary R. Collins, Christian Coaching: Helping Others Turn Potential into Reality (USA: NavPress, 2002), 359.
3 Collins, 359-360.

subject at hand."[4] Throughout the literature, the art and practice of coaching is clearly distinguished from psychotherapy, consulting, and other related support professions.

Let's look at some similarities and differences between coaching, counseling, mentoring, and consulting.

Coaching is a positive, future-oriented form of psychology which focuses on finding fulfillment, enhanced performance, team building, vision casting, career growth, and reaching one's goals and dreams. Coaching enables people to set and reach goals while focusing on the present and the future, possibilities, getting unstuck, and turning dreams into realities. In coaching sessions, the coach and the client (or friend) are equals who work together to bring about change. The best coaching is typically done with people who have training in coaching skills such as listening, asking powerful questions, and encouraging.[5]

> What oxygen is to the lungs, such
> is hope to the meaning of life.
> **—EMIL BRUNNER**

Counseling, on the other hand, often focuses on problems, dealing with conflicts, insecurities, spiritual struggles, and emotional issues such as depression, anxiety, and anger. Counseling fixes what is wrong while focusing on the causes of problems that arise from the past and

---

4 John Whitmore, Coaching for Performance: Growing Human Potential and Purpose 4th ed. (London and Boston: Nicholas Brealey Publishing, 2009), 14.
5 Collins, 16.

on bringing healing and stability. Unlike the coaching relationship, in which the coach and client are equals, the counselor is the expert who treats clients, providing healing and direction. For this reason counseling requires credentials and expertise in psychology, psychopathology, and therapeutic skills.[6]

Mentoring, while appearing to be similar to coaching, is significantly different. A mentor is typically a more senior individual who imparts knowledge and skills in the areas of wisdom, opportunities, and counsel to a more junior person. A coach builds the person's decision-making ability by asking him or her to think things through in a structured way, while the mentor teaches the person, letting him draw information from the mentor or learn from the mentor's experience. In other words, coaching is helping people learn and pull out from *within themselves,* and mentors teach the person from what is *within the mentor.*[7]

Consulting is similar to coaching; however, consultants are paid to analyze a situation and give expert advice. Consultants usually work with several groups at a time, asking questions and analyzing an organization in order to give direction in specific areas. In the business setting, a consultant can be used to analyze existing problems and practices, suggest better marketing and business strategies, and help companies and organizations to improve performance and develop future plans. They are experts at analyzing and making recommendations.[8]

Coaching, then, can be as informal as two friends helping each other tackle a problem or as formal as a professional arrangement to accomplish the client's specific goals.

---

6 Collins, 16.
7 Collins, 18.
8 Collins, 17.

COACHING AS A DISCIPLINE

DR. CHRISTOPHER BOWEN

Executive Director & Master Coach Trainer, Dream Releaser Coaching;
Founder & President, 5 Star Personal and Corporate Development

A very common question concerning coaching as a discipline is how to distinguish between the professions of consulting, counseling, and mentoring. Actually, there are very specific differences. There is a time and a place for each of these disciplines, and they cannot be substituted for each other. For example, it's not productive to coach someone that needs counseling or mentor someone who needs consulting.

The practice of a counselor is to help fix what is wrong with the client. This often zeros in on relational conflicts, anxieties, spiritual or emotional struggles, or problems that have hindered him/her to the point of seeking help. The counselor is the expert, treating the client who has an unhealthy state emotionally or mentally, and bringing them to a place of healing and direction for a brighter future. Counseling can be very complex. Therefore, it requires both credentials and expertise in therapeutic skill, psychology, and psychopathology.

A mentor is typically an experienced, mature and "senior" individual who imparts their wisdom, skills, and experiences to a "junior" person who seeks advice and information from them. Mentors teach the mentee from their wealth of knowledge and experience.

Of these three disciplines, consulting is probably most like coaching, but it is also significantly different in that consultants are paid to analyze a situation and provide expert advice. Typically, consultants work with several teams or groups at a time, asking questions, observing aspects of the organization, and giving direction in specific areas. The consultant offers recommendations and direction that assist companies, churches, or nonprofits in improving performance and reaching future success.

What distinguishes coaching from these other practices is that the coach provides a positive, future-oriented form of psychology to clients. This enables people to not only set, but reach goals, focusing on the present and future. This enables clients to realize their possibilities, get unstuck, and turn their dreams into reality. Through regular coaching sessions, the client and coach are equals, working together to bring solutions and change. A successful coach has received proper training in coaching skills, understanding and exercising skills of asking powerful questions, listening, holding the client accountable, remaining neutral, and allowing silence so the client can thoroughly process his/her thoughts. Together they celebrate even the smallest victories. The coach is always an encourager, cheering clients on to their personal goals and desired destiny.

With coaching, timing is everything. The key to success is knowing if clients are ready to be coached, or if they actually need to seek assistance from a professional counselor or another form of support first. If the client is depressed, extremely stressed, or their personal lives are falling apart, they may need to get some emotional or psychological help before pursuing their dream. Wise coaches are able to discern when professional counseling or another form of assistance is necessary for the client, and they can steer clients in the needed direction, so clients can eventually be successful with a coaching experience.

I have developed myself and my business of coaching for the highest returns by seeking clients who were determined to move forward in finding their purpose and destiny. This was obtained by building healthy relationships with my clients and moving them at a steady pace to obtain their goals. As a master coach, it is essential to provide the highest quality service to your clients. In my coaching firm, I have established certain ethics and protocols that are nonnegotiable. These include but are not limited to:

- Starting and ending sessions on time.
- Giving my undivided attention.
- Showing care and concern.
- Using integrity at all times.
- Not allowing my values to affect clients' decisions.
- Assuring my client of confidentiality.
- Asking permission to share my personal experiences, regardless of vulnerability, that can provide my clients with security.
- Moving them at their pace.
- Celebrating the small wins.

These practices have resulted in success for many of my clients, which in turn helps me gain a higher level of confidence, satisfaction, and success as a coach. As my clients find success in reaching their goals, they recommend my coaching services to individuals that I would have possibly never had the opportunity to meet otherwise.

Coaches find their "niche" in the coaching experience in different ways. I have found great satisfaction in watching my clients reach goals in their journeys to weight loss, entrepreneurship, leadership, becoming authors, financial freedom, spiritual growth, and other pursuits. In my opinion, the greatest level of success is to see my client have an "aha" moment. If I hadn't asked the right question—and listened—my client might have remained stuck.

When you find what you love so much you would do it every day for nothing, you'll know you've found your heartbeat and what will make you successful and fulfill your life and dreams. You have to "take your job and love it" so much that you cannot imagine doing anything else. This has been my journey as a coach. I have worn many hats as pastor, entrepreneur, and professor, but nothing compares to giving hope to others who have become stagnant or have lost their dreams but have found new aspiration through the coaching experience.

CHAPTER 2

THE HISTORY OF COACHING

I n the last three decades, coaching has emerged as a multidisciplinary profession. According to the literature, this modern-day surge appears to have originated through the coaching and writing of Timothy Gallwey, Harvard educator and tennis expert. According to Gallwey, a player's inner state is more of an opponent than an actual competitor on the other side of the net. Gallwey believed that a competitor is a friend if he makes you stretch and run. He first wrote the book titled *The Inner Game of Tennis*, which led to writing about other sports. [9]

The athletes he coached asked him if he could apply the same principles to business, which ultimately led to his book *The Inner Game of Work*.[10] Gallwey, Whitmore, and others teamed up to meet the growing demand for sports and business coaches. By 2008, according to Homan and Miller, at least half of Fortune 1000 organizations were providing

9 Whitmore, 9-12.
10 Whitmore, 9-12

coaching in one form or another for employees.[11] Other disciplines adopted coaching either simultaneously or shortly thereafter. A scan of internet sources reveals a wide array of coaching types including: performance, skills, career, personal or life, business, executive, sports, and health, to name a few.

Executive and business coaching is a relatively recent phenomenon, corresponding to the rise in complexity in the business world. In the past, managers and bosses could micromanage details and people, but as globalization expanded and technology increased the breadth and depth of information, people in the business world realized they needed professionals to help them cope with the multiplied pressure.

In her excellent book, *Sourcebook of Coaching History*, Vikki Brock outlines the progression of the history of coaching:

- 1930s-1950s: Psychologists and therapists began adapting their practices to work with business executives, and counseling principles were applied to help people in sales connect with potential clients more effectively.

- 1960s-1970s: Business leaders became increasingly aware that their role required a unique blend of organizational development and psychological concepts. The term "process consultation" was coined in the late '60s by Edgar Schein to describe the consultant's role of assisting clients in self-discovery and self-management.

- 1980s: *Inner Game*, a book written by Timothy Gallwey, adapted the principles and practices of coaching athletes to those who were helping executives clarify goals and take steps to meet them. In the United States and Britain, coaching businesses

---

11 Madeline Homan, and Linda J. Miller, Coaching in Organizations: Best Coaching Practices from The Ken Blanchard Companies (Hoboken, NJ: John Wiley & Sons, 2008), 4.

were established, and literature began to surface related to this new industry.

■ 1990s: Executive coaching grew exponentially as training programs, associations, and conferences became more common. By the end of the decade, many books on the subject had been published, and more people entered the coaching business. The International Coaching Federation was founded in 1992.

■ 2000s to today: Coaching executives is no longer novel. In many industries, it has become a standard practice deemed necessary to keep leaders sharp and continually hone their talents. The most recent statistics show annual revenues of $11.6 billion.[12]

Brock identifies the period when coaching expanded from the C-suite to mid-management:

Coaching emerged during the postmodern period of the late twentieth century, born of a rapidly changing socioeconomic environment and nourished by the root disciplines of psychology, business, sports, and adult education. Psychology provided many of the essential theories, as well as a practical toolset, for the emerging discipline of coaching. Business provided the first theaters of operation, a fertile field for coaching's application, growth, and diffusion. The business sector also had established tools and theories, including those which concentrated on the individual, and those focused on the organization. Individual coaching was practiced in the 1980s behind closed doors as a form of workplace counseling focused on personnel problems affecting the business as a whole, and was available only to

12 Industry Statistics, https://www.ibisworld.com/industry-statistics/market-size/business-coaching-united-states/.

executives. Coaching's movement into middle-level management offered coaching its greatest early opportunity for growth. Those who worked in organization development and management consulting, were also well positioned to expand their efforts. In the business sector, the help offered to individuals and organizations had a different focus—improving the bottom line. The results focus of business coaching emphasized metrics as a critical demonstration and justification of coaching's value.[13]

Today, coaching continues to grow as more business leaders sense the need to be equipped to deal with the complexities of the modern world. In the coming decades, we anticipate more specialization as the pool of gifted coaches expands to meet the increasing challenges in the corporate world.

CHAPTER 3

WHY PEOPLE WANT A COACH

CASE STUDY

C arl has two friends who seem to have landed from different planets. As long as Carl has known him, Rex has been a sponge, soaking in principles and practices from experts in every aspect of his life. The two of them have had dozens, probably hundreds, of rich conversations about Rex's career path, his finances, and his most important relationships. When Carl suggests a book or a podcast that might help him, there's a good chance Rex has already read it or listened to it.

Michael is the polar opposite. He has bounced from one job to another, one girlfriend to another, and one set of solutions to another, but when Carl asks him simple, open questions like, "How are things going for you?" Michael acts like Carl has threatened to kill him! He reacts, "Don't try to tell me how to run my life! I'm doing fine on my own!"

Carl isn't dim-witted. He has learned that meaningful interaction is off the table in his relationship with Michael—at least until Michael's pride is softened by a sense of desperation. So far, that hasn't happened.

Individuals come for coaching for various reasons. Some are stuck in an area of their lives and have not been able to make needed changes. Others are at a point of crisis where a change has to be made in order for life to continue with some normalcy. Still others desire personal growth and development. A few may even want coaching because they are curious: "What is this thing called coaching? Does it really work, and how can it help me?" The reasons individuals come for coaching vary; however, coaches must be skilled in determining the correct *timing*, know when to *refer*, and be equipped with the proper *resources* that are necessary at a given time.

There are two kinds of teachers: the kind that fills you with so much quail shot that you can't move, and the kind that just gives you a little prod behind and you jump to the skies.

—ROBERT FROST

Timing is everything. The precise point an individual enters the coaching process can determine success or failure. The person's readiness factor is crucial. Change does not, and in fact cannot, occur until the individual is ready. However, skillful coaching can move an individual toward change once he or she has determined the need for change.

The most common reasons people ask coaches for help are to:

- Clarify purpose: Many people feel stuck in their careers, and they want some help to identify their heartfelt purpose and look for opportunities.

- Identify strengths: Surprisingly, people may have a job simply because there was an opening, and they were marginally qualified for it. They sense they can do more—a lot more—and they need help to uncover their latent talents.

- Develop skills: People may have been promoted but feel less than confident about how to excel in the new role. They performed well at one level, but they need to develop the skills to achieve success at the next level.

- Set and achieve goals: Some individuals can readily identify their short-term and long-term goals, but they need assistance in clarifying the steps to reach them. Other people are "squishy" when it comes to goal setting; they can't seem to settle on one thing or another, so their direction isn't clear, and they don't know if they've accomplished anything.

- Overcome obstacles: Some of the difficulties people face are external—resistance from the supervisor, lack of effort or a less than stellar attitude by people on the team, or difficulties at home. Or his challenges may be internal—a lack of confidence, anger problems, or health concerns.

In a chronically leaking boat, energy devoted
to changing vessels is more productive
than energy devoted to patching leaks.
—WARREN BUFFETT

- Stimulate creativity: Quite a few leaders need someone to ask
  probing questions and help them envision new possibilities.
- Initiate action: Grand plans don't lead to great results if the
  person is immobilized by fear and doubt. Sometimes, people
  need to be held accountable for the first step . . . or the next step.
- Enlist support: Surprisingly, a lot of leaders try to do their team
  members' jobs for them. They haven't yet learned how to cast
  vision, enlist buy-in, and delegate responsibility.
- Gain confidence: People live for encouragement, and they die
  without it. A coach can be someone's biggest cheerleader.
- Get past personal pain: Though a coach doesn't play the role of
  a therapist, people are often stuck because they've experienced
  a painful past. A hope-based coaching model provides a plan to
  overcome the past, so greater success is on the horizon.
- Referral: Many people make their first appointment with a coach
  because someone made the recommendation. In fact, like most
  businesses, this is how coaches grow their practices.

Coaching may not be the answer for a particular friend or client. The
coach (or caring friend) needs to be able to discern when professional
counseling is needed or when some other form of assistance is appropriate. For instance, coaching may or may not be appropriate in a crisis

or emergency. The coach needs to be equipped to operate in a triage manner and determine what is needed and what the priority should be at any given moment. For example, coaching may be appropriate down the line, but if a person is clinically depressed or a marriage is on the edge of collapse, counseling is essential at the moment. The coach should never be reluctant to refer to a competent physician, therapist, or other professional.

For example, in a hospital emergency room, usually the receptionist or nurse exercises the practice of triage and sorts the patients. Care is then given according to the urgency of the need. A professional and accurate assessment is crucial to the individual needing care. If a person with a kidney stone is driven to the emergency room by a family member, triage protocol gives precedence to those who are transported by ambulance. Ambulance after ambulance arrives and those patients are immediately placed in a room for treatment, but the person who is driven there by her family waits in agony. In this case, the protocols of assessment and assignment of resources didn't serve this patient's needs. Similarly, a coach needs to be keenly aware of when to refer for appropriate treatment.

CHAPTER 4

PROVEN MODELS

Over the last few decades, a number of leading coaches have developed particular models that have proven to be very effective. It's instructive to take a quick glance at the more prominent ones:

THE GROW MODEL

This was developed by Sir John Whitmore in the 1980s and is one of the most popular. The process uses the metaphor of a journey:

Goal: Where do you want to go?

Reality: Where are you now?

Options: What can you do to get there?

Will: What actions will you take?

In this approach, the coach's role is to assist in clarifying the goal, so it is both inspirational and achievable.

Source: *Coaching for Performance* by John Whitmore

THE CLEAR MODEL

As an alternative to GROW, this model was developed in the early '80s by Peter Hawkins. The elements include:

Contract: Determine the outcomes, scope, and process of coaching.

Listen: The coach asks good questions, listens carefully, and nudges the conversation.

Explore: The coach and client or friend delve more deeply into the topic.

Action: The client or friend makes a commitment to take the identified steps of progress.

Review: Follow-up sessions solidify progress and clarify next steps.

OSCAR

This model focuses primarily on the solution rather than the problem. It includes:

Outcome: Determine the specific goals.

Situation: Identify the person's talents and knowledge.

Choices: Explore the various available options.

Actions: Determine the steps forward.

Reviews: Follow up to reinforce progress and make any course corrections.

Sources: *Performance Coaching Toolkit* by Will Thomas and Angus McLeod and *The OSCAR Coaching Model* by Andrew Gilbert and Karen Whittleworth

Treat people as if they were what they ought to be, and you help them become what they are capable of becoming.

—GOETHE

THE DREAM RELEASER COACHING MODEL

At Dream Releaser Coaching, our goal is to equip our coaches to help people grow and grasp their destinies. Nothing brings greater fulfillment than helping others succeed, and that is our vision. The Dream Releaser Coaching Model serves as a guide to provide the steps you need to *discover dreams*, *raise awareness*, and *coach the process*. The model is cyclical rather than linear. During the coaching process, you may find yourself moving from one stage back to another to make sure the person is satisfied with their direction and decisions. For example, at times it may be necessary to reassess the coaching agreement to confirm that expectations are being met, or as a client or friend moves into the aligning stage of the action process, you may need to allow for values to be articulated to ensure the best choices. Let's take a look at each component.

1) **Assess**
   - Connect through relationship: Establishing relational capital cultivates the atmosphere needed for the safety and security the person needs to open up about plans and goals.
   - Conduct Motivational Interviewing: Principles of motivational interviewing include expressing empathy, supporting self-efficacy, rolling with resistance, and developing discrepancy between present behavior and important personal goals or values.

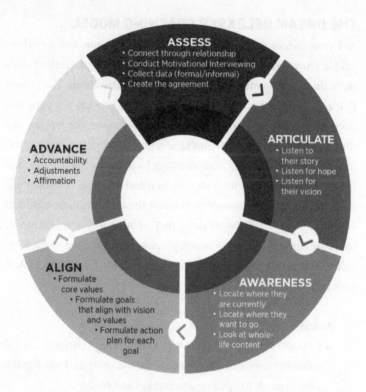

- Collect Data (formal/informal): Laying the foundation by collecting information about the person—general and specific. This can be in the form of formal assessment and/or actively listening to the friend or client.
- Create the agreement: Defining the expectations of the coaching relationship from its origination and mutually agreeing on the parameters.

2) **Articulate**
   - Listen to their story: Express your engagement in the coaching process by actively listening to people as they share their story. Assure them that you are fully concentrating on what they are conveying.
   - Listen for hope: Attentively notice when there is an expectation, ambition, desire, or goal being communicated. Be conscientious of their aspirations.
   - Listen for their vision: Encourage imagination, creativity, and dreaming out loud to support their vision.

3) **Awareness**
   - Locate where they are currently: Recognize the reality as it currently stands. Ask your friend or client to talk about the actuality of their situation.
   - Locate where they want to go: Use powerful questions to discover their desired outcome. Promote dreaming out loud and continue to provide the safe, comfortable environment for the person to do so.
   - Look at whole-life context: Ask the person to consider life at a later time based on the decisions they make at this time. Raise their awareness by encouraging the mental picture of the outcome.

4) **Align**
   - Formulate core values: Encourage the person you're coaching to discuss their core values. Determine their nonnegotiables and how the choices they're making are weighed against their values.

- Formulate goals that align with vision and values: Ask questions to ensure people's goals are aligning with their values, and bringing their vision into positive reality.
- Formulate an action plan for each goal: Set the goals into action. Urge the person to convert their dreams into working movement.

5) **Advance**

- Accountability: Allow the person to determine the amount of accountability they need to pursue these goals. Identify who will hold them accountable.
- Adjustments: Confirm the person's confidence in the direction they are heading. Provide the time and comfortable space for the one you're coaching to consider their action plan and to make adjustments, if needed.
- Affirmation: Use your earned relationship capital in the coaching relationship to confirm the person's determination. Display support and confirmation by encouraging their action plan.

Every coach—and every person who wants to use coaching principles and practices with friends and coworkers—can explore the benefits and limitations of different models to find the one that promises to be most effective.

CHAPTER 5

LIMITATIONS

CASE STUDY

When Monica walked through her front door, she walked over to the sofa and sat down heavily. Her husband, Daniel, said only, "Again?"

"Yes, again," Monica replied as she shook her head.

"How long are you going to give yourself to someone who has proven she isn't willing to do what's necessary to improve her life?"

Monica had heard that question so many times that she had a stock answer: "You don't understand. Deborah has no one else to turn to." She then went through the litany of Deborah's problems. "She has diabetes, and she has a weight problem. Her legs and feet hurt so much that she can't concentrate at work. Her parents were awful when she was growing up, so she struggles with depression. Her own children have distanced themselves from her. It's only been a year since she and her husband got divorced, and her finances are in trouble."

With very little emotion, Daniel responded, "I know you've been her friend since high school. That's a good and right role for you, but you've gone way beyond that. So . . . you're her physician, psychiatrist, therapist, and financial advisor. When did you get those credentials?"

Monica exploded, "She doesn't have anyone but me! Where would she be without me?"

"Where, indeed," Daniel whispered under his breath.

Helping people take steps to move from raw potential to new possibilities is often exhilarating, but we need to remember our limitations. Let's outline some of the most important ones:

- If people aren't willing to change, we can't make them change. As much enthusiasm, hope, and forward-focus we may have for our friends or clients, if they continually throw up roadblocks— even though they still pay us—we need to step back and have an honest talk about the efficacy of our relationship.

- If people bring up issues that are beyond our pay grade, such as a diagnosis of a personality disorder, clinical depression, or some other psychological problem, we need to make a referral to a physician or a therapist.

- If we learn about criminal activity, and the person is either the victim or the perpetrator, we need to follow the state guidelines for reporting—and we need to make the report sooner rather than later.

- In a professional coaching relationship, if the client is reluctant to pay for our services, we need to take that as a large red flag that the relationship isn't working. It's time to have an honest conversation about the perceived value of what we offer.

- It's wonderful to become friends with our clients, and in fact, if that doesn't happen something is wrong, but we need to have clear boundaries for our time and availability. For instance, don't tell people, "Call me any time," because some of them will! In the agreement, spell out your commitment and your availability— and stick to them.

All of us have limitations—of expertise and time, at least—and we need to remain mindful that overpromising and overcommitting inevitably lead to bad outcomes. Coaching is one of the most rewarding professions we can have but only if we communicate and enforce clear expectations and boundaries.

Without continual growth and progress, such words as improvement, achievement, and success have no meaning.
—BENJAMIN FRANKLIN

EVOLVING AS A COACH

MOREN ADENUBI, CCIM, CIPS, CPM
Managing Broker, Crown Realty Experts, Real Estate Instructor
& Master Coach Trainer, Dream Releaser Coaching

I truly believe that my debt to the world is to glorify God by becoming the best version of myself that I can be. One of my favorite sayings is, "Many people do not grow up; they just get older!" This is truly a tragedy. We are born with the raw materials that we need to cultivate and develop into the light that is to shine in this world. Our experiences, resources, and relationships should help shape us into better human beings. When I use the resources that I have been blessed with to discover the best in me, I get to grow and become a better person. I get to discover who God created me to be and fashion my best life.

Some of the most impactful "aha" moments in my life happened in a coaching session where I was being coached. I remember the discovery of why I had created an artificial limit on my income—that discovery came from a question my coach asked me. My answer to that question was shocking and enlightening, and ultimately, it helped me remove that barrier. That discovery did not just move me forward financially, it revealed to me that there are sometimes unknown barriers that are holding us back. Personally, discovering that, rather than reading it in a book, has made me a better coach. I can also recite several other stories to this effect.

When I was working on my last coaching certification, I had the opportunity to write my life plan. The course forced me to look at twelve areas of my life and create a map of self-improvement and accountability that prepared me for the greatest journey of my life—walking through cancer. The strength and courage that I developed and having a life plan have been invaluable to me in helping other people who face difficult circumstances.

It is easy to throw away a future that's unclear. On the other hand, when one has a clear life plan and a path to accomplish it, it provides a reason to get up with excitement every day. Developing my life plan and seeing the energy I derive from it helps me guide others. The hope I received from having a life plan and specific goals is what helped me discover my own ministry—my desire to pursue a coaching career was birthed out of this Dream Releaser Coaching course.

I have discovered that the more I get to know and accept myself, the more confident I become. I embrace both my strengths and weaknesses. I challenge myself to use every experience to grow. I get to take my masks off and truly operate in who I am—and not fool myself (or anyone else) into believing that I am someone or something other than my true self. As intimidating as it was for me when I started to embrace myself, I discovered that the more authentic I was, the more I allowed others to walk in authenticity. The more transparent I was, the more those around me were honest with me and themselves.

These are invaluable characteristics in the coaching arena as we want our coaches to bring their true selves to the table—in other words, we need to create an atmosphere of authenticity. The world teaches us to put on a persona to be accepted, and my goal is to continue to show up as I am and allow my clients as well as others to do the same, thereby fostering an environment that not only welcomes authenticity, but promotes it.

I discovered that there was joy in me even in the ups and downs (especially the downs) of life. This discovery helped me know that I wanted to help others discover their assignments and their joy. It is easier to walk people to a place of discovery when we are there ourselves. Our journeys may be different, but we can certainly use similar road maps to get there.

It is impossible to turn the darkness down. Instead, we must turn the light on. When I walk in my insecurities and fail to grow, I also cap the potential of others, not allowing them to become their best selves. I can celebrate others because, through seeing my worth, I can embrace theirs.

I truly believe that Marianne Williams said it best in her poem, "Our Deepest Fear," when she wrote, "And when we let our own light shine, we unconsciously give other people permission to do the same."

CHAPTER 6

YOUR HEART, YOUR FUTURE

You can become a great coach by asking good questions and listening more effectively. However, coaching is much more than those practices alone. We also help people set goals and craft a plan of action steps, and we offer accountability to keep them on track. Imparting skills is important, but the foundation of great coaching is what's *in your heart*. If you have the right heart, you can make mistakes in your techniques, but the friend or client will still be transformed—technique without heart is a disaster!

Effective coaching comes from a conscious imitation of other coaches—especially the person who has been your coach. Think for a moment about how your coach works with you on the change issues in your life. Before you ever intended to become a coach, something inside you wanted to reach your destiny. When you found a coach, you may not have made much progress, but you longed to reach your full potential.

Your coach had (and has) an unconditional belief in your destiny. The power of this person's faith in you empowers you to change from the inside out—because you want to, not just to look good on the outside and impress people. *This intrinsic motivation is the power of coaching.* As coaches, we imitate those who have had a profound impact on our lives, and we give people the same kind of unconditional love, unconditional support, and an unconditional belief. *We give the free gift of an unconditional relationship to people, and our confidence in them empowers them to change in ways they only dreamed possible.*

If your friend is doing something you don't understand, you can show you believe in him by not judging. Look past the exterior into the heart and believe there is a good reason for what he is doing. If the person has a problem or growth issue, he is capable of solving it. If, in your estimation, the person is making a serious mistake, don't rescue and don't control. Ask great questions to clarify choices, and invite the person into the process of self-discovery. In every situation, your first responsibility as a coach is to be a caring, understanding individual who is ultimately concerned about moving people into their full potential. The relationship comes first, and it's the relationship that enables the change.

Believing in people is what makes coaching unique. Having faith in the person's future enables us to look beyond the immediate and superficial problems and focus on untapped potential and the spark of hope within them. Coaching is an active discipline. Trust in the components and processes of coaching to move people toward their destiny.

If we have the faith to coach a person, we believe we can take our hands *off* their lives, encourage them to think and see like never before, and they will eventually get a clear picture of a desired future. In an environment of honesty, support, and optimism, something incredible will take place—transformation will begin.

The problem with faith in people is that you can't fake it. As you start your experience, you can't just believe unconditionally in all of your friends or clients. Beliefs don't tend to change by force of will. It is like telling yourself that you won't be angry or that your past has not hindered your future. Sometimes, the more you try to believe something, the harder it is to have real faith.

But there is a simple, effective way to strengthen your belief in people. It is *practicing the disciplines of believing in people.* When we discipline ourselves to do practical things to move people forward, cloudy situations gradually (or suddenly) become clear, healing begins, and progress is realized.

Coaching involves several disciplines such as listening, asking questions, and holding others accountable. Listening is more than just a good technique—it's a practical way of saying, "I believe in you!" Really, "I'm-100 %-here-right-now" listening sends a message to people that they are very important to you. Listening sends the message, *What you are saying is so valuable that I'm going to put aside all my own thoughts and agenda just to focus on* you. To really listen is to say in unmistakable language, *I believe in you.* In a practical sense, listening *is* believing in a person.

Asking questions is also very important. The technique of asking powerful questions and awaiting answers with follow-up questions increases a person's ownership of the process, and it makes them responsible for their own solutions. Great questions have significant benefits. Our questions clarify a person's goals and values (for her and for us). Asking questions is an unmistakable way of saying, *I believe in your capacity and your ability! You can do it!*

> If you hang out with chickens, you're
> going to cluck, and if you hang out
> with eagles, you're going to fly.
> —STEVE MARABOLI

Some of us are more passionate than others, but all of us care about something. All of us have moments when our hearts race, our blood pressure spikes, and our adrenaline pumps. However, some people don't know how to channel their passions in ways that produce genuine fulfillment.

As a coach, you have the opportunity to help people identify their passions and connect their innate drive to their life's purposes. Questions cause people to think.

- "Who are you most interested in serving and shaping?" This question invites them to identify the specific target group they want to influence, including interns, spouses, the elderly, youth, students, entrepreneurs, young children, divorced people, single mothers, and widowers, among other categories. Thinking outside of themselves allows them to "walk in another person's shoes" and brings clarity to the *who*.

- "What do you love to do? What activities feed and fulfill your passion?" Surprisingly, many people have never considered these questions. They've been committed to doing what had to be done, but they've seldom thought about what brings enjoyment and fulfillment. The scope of this question isn't limited to their careers. Relationships, service organizations, hobbies, sports, travel, and any other interest could contribute to their life's purpose. When friends or clients answer these questions, they may realize they can devote more time to interesting, inspiring activities, and they can weave these things into their lives more effectively.

- "When did you feel the strongest, and what were you doing?" When people reflect on this question, they identify skills and recall experiences that made them feel empowered and purposeful.
- "When have you felt genuinely fulfilled?" Some people have been under stress so long they don't recall ever feeling fulfilled. Most people don't have to think very hard to recall meaningful experiences. Identifying past positive experiences can point the way to a renewed hope for the future.
- "When you were a child, what did you want to be when you grew up?" This question touches on convergence. It helps people see the connections between childhood hopes, present opportunities, and future dreams.

Sometimes the challenge isn't helping people discover their passions. They know what excites and motivates them. The challenge is helping them realize their passions are the fuel of growth and progress. The engine of their lives can't go very far without them! They also need to realize they are unique individuals. They can't borrow the passions of a parent, boss, or spouse. They have to identify their own and learn to live by them.

CASE STUDY

Amanda is a loving wife and mother who takes great pride in her home. She grew up with a hardworking father and a homemaker mother. Every day she returned from school to a homemade snack. She sat at the table with her mom to complete her homework and replay the day's events. She often worked alongside her mom in the kitchen to cook dinner, and she looked forward to hearing the door open, so she could greet her dad after work. Throughout Amanda's middle and high school years, her mom was deeply involved in field trips, classroom parties, and weekly lunches.

Amanda wanted to be just like her mom when she grew up. She wanted her kids to experience the same love she felt from her mom, and she wanted her husband to have a happy, refreshing home when he returned from work each day. She wanted to be just like her mother—a loving, caring, happy, devoted wife and mom.

Years later, Amanda got married. She and her husband had two children of their own. She poured love into them every day. She made their lunches, had snacks ready when they got home from school, and spent afternoons in the park with them. Amanda exuded love and devotion for her family, but something was missing. She remembered seeing her mom's genuine expressions of contentment, but she couldn't quite find that point of satisfaction in her role as a wife and mom. After talking things over with her husband, she began to look for meaningful work. She wanted a career outside the home.

After a few weeks, Amanda found a part-time job as the receptionist in a rehabilitation center. She loves her work. She encourages patients' families when they come to visit their loved ones. She has never found such fulfillment. In this role, Amanda feels deeply satisfied, and she knows what she's doing is important. She isn't neglecting her children or her husband. She sees the kids off to school before work and is there to meet the bus when they return home. The housework suffers a little, but all in all, things are getting accomplished. The kids help out with the meals, and her husband agrees that the financial support has been a source of relief for him.

On the surface, things couldn't be going better for Amanda, but something is still wrong. Amanda is plagued with feelings of guilt. She doesn't feel that she measures up to being the perfect mother and wife—the mother and wife her mom was. She wonders why it takes something other than serving her beautiful children and loving husband to bring her satisfaction. She accuses herself of being selfish, as if having her own passions in life is somehow a fatal flaw. In fact, she sees herself as a colossal failure.

If you were Amanda's coach, how would you help her?

Every person is passionate about a specific role, and everyone is equipped with a specific gifting. Several key components shape our talents and abilities.

Genetics and family history are important. If one of your parents is talented in engineering, you may have inherited similar abilities. If a parent excelled in sports, you may have inherited athletic prowess. If your mom or dad is a singer, you may be interested in music. Many of our natural talents and abilities are a direct result of the gene pool.

It's difficult, though, to distinguish between *nature* and *nurture*. Sometimes, we develop interests and talents simply by living with people who display particular passions and abilities. If you are taught as a young person how to value and handle money, these lessons probably follow you into adulthood. Being mentored by an exceptional coach or teacher during the teen years can produce an impressive gift of leadership as you grow older. Learning to become an active listener can develop the gift of communication: knowing when to listen and when to speak.

In order to live a fulfilled life, we have to discover our gifts as well as our passions—and hopefully, they complement each other. Many people waste much of their lives wishing they had this person's talents or that person's skills. They want to sing that well, or be that intelligent, or communicate that eloquently. Comparison—especially negative comparison—poisons hearts and erodes confidence.

When you embrace your gift, you begin to *think* differently. Instead of longing to be like someone else, you embrace your own talents and let them shine. You begin to *live* differently because you are no longer comparing yourself to others and feeling disappointed. You devote time and other resources to sharpen and use your gift. You *believe* differently because you value yourself and realize you can make a significant and unique impact.

You have the opportunity and responsibility to develop your talents, abilities, and gifts. Your personality affects how you approach your abilities. If you're an extrovert, you have little problem stepping into new situations and volunteering for an assignment. Introverts may have consummate talents, but often they are reluctant to volunteer.

Past experiences affect the development of your gift. Successes usually create confidence that you will be effective, but past failures may cause a fear that keeps you from trying something new. Those who have been affirmed and validated in the past have a firm platform to take risks, but those who feel insecure are afraid of failure and rejection.

Affirmation makes a difference—to you and to your friends or clients. If you have been encouraged to believe in yourself, you will embrace your gift and take the risk to use it for the benefit of others. You will believe that you have something that's special, something worth releasing.

Our abilities and gifts are treasures, and we are accountable for how we invest them. We must identify them, own them, and use them wisely. Our talents aren't neutral. They are sources of great power. We can use them for good or for wrong purposes. If we don't find a sense of balance, we can invest everything in our abilities, become exhausted, and burn out. Or we can use our talents to gain power over others instead of serving them. Based on the motive, a person's gift can be a wonderful strength or a tragic weakness.

To use our gifts wisely, we need clear boundaries. Any good thing can be misused. When we are too dedicated to our careers, advancement, power, or money, we use our talents for selfish purposes—and everybody gets hurt. We need to look at our motives, how we use our time, and our impact on others. What do we hope to accomplish by using our gifts? If we primarily want to further our careers, we may gain a lot of power, but we'll crush people on our way to the top. How much time are we investing in our talents? If we can't stop thinking about our work, we've lost perspective. Then, our gifts own us instead of us using them. And what impact are we having on those around us? Do they feel valued and respected, or do they feel neglected and used?

Comparison inevitably produces a perceived *value differential*—we feel inferior to those who seem to be more skilled and talented, and we feel superior to those who aren't as sharp as we think we are. Inferiority and superiority are two sides of the same coin—insecurity. When we have a deep sense of inherent value, we don't have to compare. We can applaud others who succeed because we're genuinely happy for their success, and we can give comfort to those who are hurting because we truly care.

In the business world, families, and friendships, our gifts often produce both applause and criticism. People around us may use applause out of authentic appreciation, and they may criticize us to help us improve, but many others are insecure. They use applause to "suck up" to us, and they use criticism to tear us down. Remember that insincere praise and harsh critiques come from insecure people. Their insecurities are no different than ours. Examine your heart, and learn to work, give, love, and serve for right reasons—no matter how much praise or condemnation you receive.

Gifts are dangerous without guiding principles and good boundaries. Motives matter. We need to dig deep in our hearts to wrestle with our insecurities, so we develop right reasons to do good things. Many people have plenty of drive, but few are genuinely humble. Know how your gifts can be beneficial to others, and strive to use them for that purpose.

It's a daunting task to address insecurities, expose hidden motives, and wrestle with comparison, but it's essential. As we become more secure, we become open to see blind spots, we feel free from the bondage of performance, we avoid burnout, and we enjoy life much more. Boundaries allow you to soar in your gifts—but with discipline that ensures you value others in the process.

Coaches have enormous privileges and specific responsibilities. The privileges include:

- Seeing destiny fulfilled in others' lives
- Watching transformation take place
- Self-gratification by seeing others reach their potential

- Subsidiary income
- Working for yourself
- Setting your own schedule
- Relaxed atmosphere
- Reaching your destiny in life
- Empowering others to change their perspectives
- Gaining permission to speak into other's lives in order for them to discover truth
- Being the conduit through which the answers flow
- Having access into the dreams of another's life
- Gaining the trust of individuals as they open up their deepest thoughts
- Assisting others in uncovering patterns and repeat behaviors that need to be adjusted

And the responsibilities are:
- Accountability
- Encouragement
- Punctuality
- Moving at the pace of the one you're coaching
- Authenticity
- Honesty
- Realistic support
- Self-discovery—allow others to set the agenda,
- Modeling integrity
- Being a person of your word
- Coaches' lives should exemplify what they expect of others
- Providing an atmosphere of secured confidentiality

- Providing a safe place for openness
- Being vulnerable to share your own experience to build relational capital with others
- Asking permission to speak into someone's life
- Probing and sifting to reach the deeper issues possibly being evaded
- Listening with other-centered intent, not self-centered
- Correctly representing the beliefs and core values of the coaching company

Is coaching right for you? You've obviously been thinking about becoming a coach, and you may have been dreaming of what it would be like to have a powerful impact on people who ask you to help them fulfill their dreams. You care about people, your friends say you help them a lot, you've overcome your own struggles, and you're curious about whether you have what it takes to be a competent coach. You're in a really good place!

Look at this inventory to gauge your interest and talents:
Rate each of these qualities on a scale of 0 (nonexistent) to 10 (outstanding):

_____ People look to me when they need advice or feel stuck.

_____ I'm known as a good listener.

_____ I've learned some lessons the hard way.

_____ I'm passionate about my own development.

_____ I love to see others succeed.

_____ I'm dependable. People say they can count on me.

_____ When people are in trouble, I'm both patient and persistent.

_____ I have a knack for seeing potential in others.

_____ I'm willing and eager to launch this as a business.

_____ I know when I'm in too deep with someone's problems.

_____ **Total score**

Scoring:

0-20 Put the book down. This isn't for you—and you know it!

21-40 You have some relational skills, but probably not enough to be a successful coach.

41-60 You're probably either a very compassionate person or a very disciplined person, but maybe not both.

61-80 You have a lot of the talents and heart necessary to be a great coach, and this is a real possibility for you.

81-100 You're incredibly gifted and skilled in interpersonal connections, and you'll be a terrific coach—or you lack a measure of self-understanding. Ask your spouse or your best friend (the honest one) to take this inventory with you in mind, and see if your observations are confirmed.

If you're interested in learning what it means to be an effective coach, keep reading, keep asking great questions, and keep dreaming of what this would look like for you and your future.

PART 2

The Purpose of Coaching

CHAPTER 7

UNLOCKING GOALS
AND DREAMS

James J. Braddock, also known as *The Cinderella Man* in the days of America's Great Depression, displayed such determination that he became a hero and a symbol of hope to the hopeless. In a modern-day movie titled "Cinderella Man," he is depicted as a poverty-stricken, washed-out prizefighter who was reduced to the lowermost point of his life. Finding himself in financial ruin—the recipient of public relief, on the verge of losing his family, and with no one believing in his ability to make a comeback—Braddock mustered a determination from within that could not be extinguished. Seeing his comeback in the ring as an avenue to win back and provide for his family, against all odds, he returned to the ring. Suddenly, the ordinary working man became the mythic athlete. Carrying the hopes and dreams of the disenfranchised on his shoulders, Braddock rocketed through the ranks until this underdog chose to do the unthinkable: take on the heavyweight champ of the world, the unstoppable Max Baer, renowned for having killed two men in the ring."[14]

The night of the big event came. Fans of Braddock gathered in churches and in various small groups crouched around buzzing, heated radios to listen to the blow-by-blow. Those who could scraped up a few dollars to bid on their hero. It was a full-length, nail-biting fight to the finish. Ironically, it was Braddock's adversity that had best prepared him for the fight of his life. He had injured one hand severely, but in order to keep his job as a day laborer and provide for his family he had to do as much work using his one good hand as other men did using both. Throughout the fight, his opponent, Max Baer, barraged him with punches above and below the belt—physically and mentally.

Braddock persevered using the thoughts and dreams of a brighter future for his family for motivation. It was all he could do to garner his wife's support. She didn't want her husband to be Baer's third victim. He told her, "I can't do this without your support," so she offered her support just moments prior to the beginning of the fight. There was no knock out, so the world waited for the judges' tally, and then the answer came, "The winner and *new . . .*" and that was enough verbiage for the waiting world to erupt in pandemonium.[15]

One of the most refreshing things about coaching is that we are tour guides on the person's "journey of self-discovery." The solution to the problem area is actually resolved by the friend or client. You are simply assisting in the discovery that their answers lie within themselves, so you never even have to let your opinions or feelings become involved

---

14 Sujit R. Varma, "Plot Summary for Cinderella Man," 2005, http://www.imdb.com/title/tt0352248/plotsummary, accessed 10 July, 2012.
15 For the complete story, rent or buy Cinderella Man.

in the process. By asking the right questions, you steer them in the direction they need to go to reach their goals.

Powerful questions are the key to successful coaching. However, many inexperienced coaches struggle to formulate them. Great questions are like gold: incredibly valuable but very rare. Many of us go through our days asking questions that require very little reflection. People only respond, "Yes," "No," or "Fine." We live at such a fast pace that we don't want to take time to know more than we have to!

In coaching, however, the ability to ask penetrating questions is essential to uncover hidden desires, clarify goals, and build relationships of trust and respect. Like all skills, learning to ask powerful questions takes time, training, and practice. Instead of asking, "How much weight did you lose this week?" we learn to invite deeper reflection: "Tell me what happened with your weight loss goals for the week."

Don't ask closed-ended questions like these:

- Have you made any progress this week?
- Have you improved your relationship with your coworker this week?
- Are there obstacles blocking your goal?
- Would you like to give this a try?
- Do you need someone to hold you accountable for this decision?
- Are you willing to take the next step?
- Would you like to talk?
- Do you have other options?
- Do you see this going anywhere?
- Is this decision congruent with your values?

Instead, ask open-ended questions:

- Tell me about your progress this week.
- What steps have you taken to improve your relationship with your coworker this week?
- What obstacles are blocking your goal?
- What steps can you take to get started?
- Who can hold you accountable for this decision?
- What are the next steps you are willing to take?
- Say more about that.
- What other options can you think of?
- Where do you see this going?
- How is this decision congruent with your values?

Creativity is especially expressed in the ability to make connections, to make associations, to turn things around and express them in a new way.

—TIM HANSEN

The examples of powerful questions and conversation starters are endless. Here are some others that have proven to be very helpful:

"What's it like to (be in your role, feel this pressure, work with this person, etc.)?"

"What's the best (or worst) outcome if you go in that direction?"

"If it doesn't work out the way you hope, what options will you have?"

"What are your fears? What makes you hesitant?"

"How can you solidify and reinforce what you're learning?"

"What will you do next time?"

"What are some resources you can lean on?"

And the one that is always pure gold: "Tell me more about that."

To reiterate, our role as coaches isn't to tell people how to run their lives. Our task is to facilitate self-understanding and self-discovery. This is accomplished by asking great questions, listening carefully, asking follow-up questions, and affirming the person's sense of direction. German pastor Dietrich Bonhoeffer was a leader of the resistance against the Nazis in World War II, and he was a gifted leader of his church. He noted, "It is the nature, and the advantage, of strong people that they can bring out the crucial questions and form a clear opinion about them. The weak always have to decide between alternatives that are not their own." Let's be strong people, and let's help the people we coach become stronger.

The greatest day in your life and mine is when we take total responsibility for our attitudes. That's the day we truly grow up.
—JOHN C. MAXWELL

UNLOCKING GOALS AND DREAMS

MAURY DAVIS
CEO, Maury Davis Coaching; Master Coach
Trainer, Dream Releaser Coaching

love a good dream. I enjoy being around dreamers who don't allow anything to distract them from their dreams. My soul is filled with happiness, joy, and fulfillment when a dream comes to fruition. I started my journey with Christ at eighteen years old with seemingly unattainable dreams. At sixty-five, those dreams are now wonderful memories. After twenty-eight years as a pastor, I was able to look down at written, tangible dreams and marvel at how dreams of an improbable future became historical fact. As I resigned my church, I shared that thought with my children. My heart was full of hope that their dreams would become fulfilled memories, too.

A key facet in attaining my dreams was the power of *coaching*. Leadership has been a buzz word for many years, but coaching can accomplish for individuals what concrete leadership principles never will. Leadership is critical to organizational growth, but leadership is static without coaching to develop the individuals. Coaching is fluid growth, movement forward, an evolution of mind and spirit that changes and cultivates great leaders.

A perfect example is when Christ gave His disciples the dream of being fishers of men. Over the 3.5 years they had together, Jesus asked questions and shared thought-provoking parables, allowing them to experience mental and spiritual enlightenment. Lessons gained through experience are more concrete than lessons imparted only verbally. They never forgot. He was a Master visionary and example of the power of coaching.

Walking people through the complicated process of achieving dreams is both challenging and fulfilling. You realize that what they are saying with their mouths is only a droplet compared to the mighty waters of a dream you sense in their hearts. That's the moment you become their coach.

I have observed coaching as it helped many people who have hired me to take the journey with them. There are two types of people. Some believe they want to be coached, they want you to help them, but they are very reticent to change perspective or thought processes. They stand unchanging in their thought no matter how many graphs, charts, pictures, clear and compelling statistics, stories of life experience, professional experience, and personal accomplishments you are qualified to share. Even though they intuitively know they are stuck and want to move forward, they don't possess the emotional or mental health to have someone speak into their lives and leadership. *Giving up control is the barrier.* Simply delivering information is inadequate in producing growth—but coaching is the miracle worker. The power of a question is greater than teaching, charting, and creating graphs. Clients grow internally when they realize answers were there all along, latent and unrecognized in their souls. A timely question, allowed to sit and marinate in a quiet moment can achieve more than an hour of persuasive arguments. Coaching elevates people's receptivity to significant change. Coaching makes change palatable by reducing it to achievable moments.

The power of a question is underestimated. Jesus asked over three hundred questions. He asked Peter who he thought He was, and Peter gained a revelation. He declared, "You are the Christ, the Son of the Living God." Christ could have just told Peter the answer, but inner-revelation is more permanent than external education. Peter gave his life for this one, cemented belief.

Recently, I was coaching a pastor who was struggling with his identity. He was entrenched in the transition from decades of being the lead pastor to passing the baton to the next. His struggle was palpable. The insecurity of "what do I do now if I'm not leading" colored every decision. Decisions made out of fear, grief, and confusion lead to unnecessary pain. My question to him was, "Are you pastoring the church, or are you pastoring the transition?" He sat quietly for a moment before the light came on as realization hit. He had a thorough revolution, a perspective shift, and an attitude change. One question changed his life.

Study the dynamics of questions. Are you skilled at questions that are diagnostic, empathetic, mission-centric, entertaining, or creative? The types of questions and delivery are endless. The most important and pro-lific questions allow a person not to be led into a solution, but to discover their own answer. Open-ended questions are a wellspring of innovation, the result of finding these suppressed answers. A coach brings a question highlighted by personal experience, character, and thought process. These internal answers are likewise altered by a person's experiences, integrity, personality, and knowledge. Bringing differing perspectives to a problem is formidable. A *good* question can change a decision, but a *great* question can change the world.

I experienced a profound sense of loss when I left my pastorate, my church, and my expanded family that I had done life with for over twenty-seven years. There were weddings and funerals and babies and jobs and motorcycle rides and laughter and tears. It was my life. When I left, I lost my historical purpose, my relational equity, and my comfort zone. I was overcome with grief and believed I would never find a role where I felt as needed or as valuable or as helpful as being a pastor.

Coaching revolutionized my experience and was able to make my per-ceived losses stepping-stones to a new season. Drawing on that pivotal moment in my life, I can look into the eyes of the next generation who is beaten up by circumstances, gossip, and frustration—so focused on the trees that they can't see the forest. As a coach, I can help them not only lead again, but lead better and stronger. Intentional, open-ended questions summon internal answers that tangibly change posture, eye contact, and hope. The collective experience of frustration, a problem, questions, reflection, and a solution yields physical effects. Not only does coaching produce a better leader with the capacity and confidence to evolve and grow and dream again, but it also provides new insight for the coach to take to the next client who feels his life and career are locked in a vault. If there is a dream to be had, there is potential to unlock.

CHAPTER 8

BUILDING HOPE

CASE STUDY

Sarah was known for her sunny optimism, but in recent weeks, her demeanor had changed. Rachel, a good friend, noticed and asked her to stop over for some coffee. It didn't take long for Sarah to spill her disappointment. Tears came to her eyes when she told Rachel, "I'm a failure. A colossal failure. My brother started his own business and is doing great, but I can't seem to get anywhere. I had dreams of writing a successful screenplay, but the feedback I got from a professional was that it was, well, trash. Then I got a dead-end job, and my relationship with Tony dried up. A few months ago, I had a vision of a great future, but now . . . I'm a complete defect!"

Rachel knew that it wasn't time for "the right answer" that would solve every problem in Sarah's life. It was time to share a shoulder for Sarah to cry on, and sooner or later, they could begin talking about finding a speck of light in the dark tunnel of Sarah's multiplied disappointments.

Allowing your past to dictate your future is a common and crippling problem for many people. It can crush a person's sense of hope . . . but it doesn't have to. Sooner or later, virtually all of us endure dire circumstances beyond our control; the way we respond to those either drags us backwards or propels us forward. We could list many kinds of difficulties that have been anchors holding people back. Failure to resolve and grow from a painful relationship from your past often affects your choices in the future. You aren't able to see your potential, and you begin to believe that you deserve nothing better than an unhealthy relationship. It creates a pattern of contradicting values. Similarly, the inability to cope with weight issues throughout your life and being unable to make a consistently positive change can result in a rollercoaster of losing and gaining weight. With hope, wonderful things are possible; without it, life is a series of dead ends and disappointments.

Barbara has a beautiful voice and plays keyboard. She is extremely creative and even paints occasionally. There is no end to her gifting. She has been with the same company for many years, and although she hasn't been promoted, she has received consistent praise for a job well done. She has a beautiful daughter and five grandchildren. Everything about Barbara's life indicates an abundantly full life; however, she lived through a devastating divorce ten years ago and still continues to go to counseling twice a month. The counseling offers a safe place to release her emotions, but it doesn't provide the push she needs to move forward in her life. She has many friendships but can't seem to remain very close to any one specifically because she has a tendency to be sour even when she's having lunch with a friend. She has so much going for her, but can't seem to focus on the assets of her life.

Barbara's past is still dictating her present, and it clouds her future. She longs for a new romantic relationship, but she can't seem to stop comparing everyone with her former husband, Peter. She remembers having so many dreams but can't seem to imagine those coming true with anyone besides Peter. She doesn't know how to step forward onto a new path, so she sabotages many new opportunities by blaming her failed marriage. It has simply become too easy for her to continue to cast blame than to take ownership of circumstances and learn from them.

Barbara is afraid to be herself. Being a couple was all she knew, and she feels she isn't smart enough or pretty enough to have a new relationship or follow through with her dreams. Instead of sifting through the hurt in search of healing, she has allowed resentment to steal her dreams. She has settled for a mediocre life when she could have one of new beginnings and romantic companionship. She pictures herself painting beautiful canvases and creating beautiful music, but the most she can do is maintain a relationship with her daughter and go to work every day. She forfeits a life of potential by refusing to face reality and change her perceptions.

It's not too much to say that hope is the essential fuel of a meaningful life. With it, we can overcome obstacles and achieve remarkable things; without it, we're left in a morass of emptiness, self-pity, and resentment.

Jürgen Moltmann's personal story as soldier and prisoner of war during World War II illustrates the power of hope. Before he was captured, Moltmann experienced numerous rigors and humiliations as a young soldier in the German army. In his autobiography, he described how he was forced to perform pointless, exhaustive exercises day after day. In February of 1945, he realized the Germans were losing the war. Hungry, thirsty, dirty, covered with lice, and with no other option, he surrendered to an English soldier. In his prison camp memoirs, he noted, "As a general rule, the prisoners with hope had the best chance of survival." He was prisoner of war until his release in April 1948. Two experiences—a friendly encounter with Scottish men and their families at the prison camp and the receipt of a Bible—propelled Molt-mann from depression to a new hope during his imprisonment. Molt-mann reflected,

The Scottish overseers and their families were the first who came to meet us, their former enemies, with a hospitality that profoundly shamed us. We heard no reproaches, we experienced a simple and warm common humanity which made it possible for us to live with the past of our own people, without repressing it and without growing callous. True, we had numbers on our backs and prisoners' patches on our trousers, but we felt accepted as people. This humanity in far-off Scotland made human beings of us once more. We were able to laugh again.

The British YMCA set up an educational camp to train teachers and Protestant pastors for post-war Germany. Moltmann was one of the prisoners allowed to study theology. Suddenly, the "[i]ntellectual worlds that had been forbidden . . . opened up." He had spent more than five years in barracks, camps, dugouts, and bunkers, but these hardships and privations formed the backdrop for the bright light of genuine hope. He reflected, "What looked at the beginning like a grim fate became an undeserved blessing. . . . We were all there with wounded souls, and when we went away, 'my soul was healed.'"[16]

The most effective way of helping people find hope is to ask a series of questions that prompts them to see hope. Imagining possibilities, considering opportunities and options, and daring to see ahead will breed hope. The following questions are suggestions. We are never to assume how the questions will be answered because every person is unique, but consider these questions.

- "If you could envision your life full of fulfilled dreams, tell me how that looks. Don't hold back; this is your dream." (These types of questions allow the person to get outside of their closed box . . . to imagine if their past weren't holding them back, what their life would look like.)

- "What do you believe is stopping you from being able to realize those dreams?" (This presents the reality, the stress point, or the snag. There is nothing wrong with allowing the person to become angry or emotional when they realize how their past has controlled and robbed them. That's powerful fuel to promote change!)

- "What will your life be like a few months from now if you don't make the decision to move forward from this past?" (This question presents the danger of remaining in bondage to the past.)

- "When you consider your dream, do you see yourself as valuable and deserving of this dream? Why or why not?"

- "What have you allowed to steal your sense of self-worth? What has happened to rob you of this hope?"

The point of these questions is to help people identify the blockage caused by unresolved pain from the past, and then to have them

---

16 Jürgen Moltmann, A Broad Place, translated by Margaret Kohl (Minneapolis: Fortress Press, 2008), 28-30.

vividly imagine the future without that baggage. This propels them into hopeful thinking.

According to C. R. Snyder, genuine hope is created and sustained through two powers: willpower and waypower. His definition of will-power is "a reservoir of determination and commitment that we can call on to help move us in the direction of the goal to which we are attending at any given moment . . . and it consists of thoughts such as *I can, I'll try, I'm ready to do this, and I've got what it takes*." Waypower, according to Snyder, "reflects the mental plan or road maps that guide hopeful thought . . . and is the driving force in hopeful thinking."[17]

Living with the nagging fear that you will never reach your goal throws you into a downward spiral of discouragement and hopeless-ness. Soon, it doesn't make sense to even try again. Believing in yourself enough to expect great things is a learned process. If you have been bat-tered and beaten down for years as a child and as an adult, new, positive thoughts need to replace the old, negative ones. Choosing to believe that your life can never be any different robs you of an opportunity to live a full life, one of realized potential.

Keys to feeding hope include bringing past hopes and successes into the present and changing ANTS into PETS. Anthony Grant and Jane Greene offer the concept of exchanging ANTS and PETS. ANTS are the Automatic Negative Thoughts that one has while PETS are Performance-Enhancing Thoughts.[18]

ANTS are Automatic Negative Thoughts.

PETS are Performance-Enhancing Thoughts.

17 C. R. Snyder, The Psychology of Hope: You Can Get There from Here, (New York: Free Press, 1994), 6.
18 Anthony Grant and Jane Greene, It's Your Life. What Are You Going to Do with It? (Great Britain: Pearson Education Limited, 2004), 128.

Hope is faith holding out its hand in the dark.
—GEORGE ILES

CASE STUDY

A bride, Donna, brought existing self-esteem issues into her marriage to Bill. She had lived a battered and beaten-down life from childhood. She was the daughter of an alcoholic parent and had never received unconditional love. All throughout the dating process, she had a hard time trusting Bill. Yet, feeling that love would overcome all the obstacles, the couple entered marriage. Bill was an outgoing go-getter who almost always accomplished his goals, won friends, and influenced the masses. He had contact with prominent people, including many strikingly beautiful and talented women. Donna couldn't handle his relationships with these women. She was jealous and suspicious. Her inadequacies and fears ate at her constantly. When they dated, she had been afraid of losing Bill to her perceived competition, and then she was even more terrified of losing her husband to them. She often accused Bill of having extramarital relationships or at least desiring to.

The situation created an unhealthy atmosphere of fighting and tears. Bill's emotions became bruised. He had tried to love Donna, but she was incapable of receiving his affection and assurances. At a point of desperation, he asked Donna, "Can you just think of me as a good man? When you have thoughts of me with another woman could you please replace them with, *Bill is a good man! I know he wouldn't be unfaithful and hurt me*"? They reached a compromise where Donna was allowed to ask Bill about his appointments and make statements ahead of time. She told him, "Please be careful. You have an appointment with so-and-so today." He graciously allowed this entrée into his calendar and even encouraged the remarks. He used them as a form of accountability. In time, Donna's negativity turned to positivity. She learned to trust Bill and receive his love. Her thoughts were completely reversed. Her questions and cautions for Bill became fewer and fewer. Her ANTS were replaced with PETS.

It's important to continually spur hope. This can be done by taking time in each session to encourage and offer support. Taking a moment to express your belief in your client or friend and pride in their accomplishments often propels them to take the next step—and it cements your relationship. Our relationship with the friend or client isn't meant to be clinical. There is more to coaching than setting action steps and checking off a list of goals that have been met. It is about empowering them to believe in themselves and to achieve things they never dreamed possible. During the meat of the session, there is nothing more powerful than listening. But the beginning and end of a session should be dripping with hope and encouragement. If you believe they can, they will be more likely to believe it, too. After all, they have faith in you, or they wouldn't have hired you to coach them. If they sense that you trust they can achieve their goals, they will be increasingly hopeful.

Those we coach also need additional encouragement and accountability outside the coaching relationship. You are responsible for encouraging the person, but you are not required to take on the responsibility for the entire accountability process. In the beginning of every coaching relationship, establish a trusting environment, and then encourage the person to find a person who can offer additional encouragement and accountability.

CHAPTER 9

FORWARD-FOCUSED COACHING

nlike counseling methods which focus on finding the root causes of behavioral problems and conflicts, coaching looks forward to hopes, goals, and dreams. Although it may be important to identify and understand past influences which may cause people to respond in certain ways, focusing on the past can unnecessarily hinder us from moving ahead.

Forward-focused coaching takes attention off the events people can't change and helps them realize they still can control their hopes and dreams for the future. It's a fact: Our response to life's events makes the difference, rather than the events themselves. For example, two children may grow up in the same household with an alcoholic parent. One child may turn to alcohol to cope with the stress and uncertainty in the family, but the other may decide to completely abstain from alcohol. Just as the rearview mirror of our cars is much smaller than the windshield, so it is with life. Coaching focuses on what's in front of our friend or client rather than what's behind them.

The coaching model embraces the philosophy and methodology of J. L. Walter and J. E. Peller's work called Solution-Focused Brief Therapy Model (SFBTM), though not at the therapeutic/counseling level. In the Solution-Focused Brief Therapy Model, the focus is shifted from the problem to the solution. Little or no attention is given to the past, a psychopathological diagnosis, the person's history, or other forms of information gathering. Attention focuses on the present and the future. The solution-focused approach optimistically assumes that people are healthy and competent, and that they can freely choose the goals they want to pursue. The coach helps people discover and develop competencies they already possess.[19][20]

Getting over a painful experience is much like crossing monkey bars. You have to let go at some point in order to move forward.
—C. S. LEWIS

One of the distinguishing features of the SFBTM is the coach's ability to identify "exception behavior." The person's problem does not occur all the time, so effort is placed on identifying exception behavior which

---

19 Gerald Corey, Theory and Practice of Counseling and Psychotherapy, 7th ed. (Belmont, CA: Brooks/Cole-Thomson Learning, 2005), 388.
20 J. L. Walter and J. E. Peller, Recreating Brief Therapy: Preferences and Possibilities (New York: Norton, 2000), quoted in Corey, 390.

leads to positive blaming of whoever is responsible for the exception.[21] An individual with a bad habit does not engage in the bad behavior 100% of the time; therefore, focus on the exception and not the rule. That is, the negative behavior (the rule) is deemphasized by focusing on times the negative behavior is not present (the exception). For instance, an alcoholic is not always intoxicated or acting out, so focus on what the individual does well or the benefits of not engaging in the negative behavior.

Many people are stuck in the past. When they think about taking steps forward in any area of life, the pain and failures of the past raise their heads as snarling monsters. Most people shrink back and fear they'll suffer even more pain if they try to move ahead in their lives. Through the tools of coaching, these ugly monsters can be put to rest once and for all. By focusing on what's ahead rather than what is behind, people can actually learn how to use failures and disappointments to catapult them into the future!

We can all name people who have used their past as an excuse for not accomplishing anything in life. The circumstances we were born into, forced into as children, or mistakes we've made as adults don't have to dictate our future. Living under the power of the past is an easy hole to fall into; it's a trap trying to hold us captive. However, ask successful people how they rose to the top, and most of them will point to a pivotal choice when they determined that their past would no longer dictate their future!

Bad things happen to good people. It is a fact of life. Our response to those bad experiences ultimately determines if we reach our desired destiny. In fact, the stories of people overcoming horrible situations

---

21 James Slate Fleming and Bill Rickord, "Solution-Focused Brief Therapy: One Answer to Managed Mental Health Care," The Family Journal: Counseling and Therapy for Couples and Families 5, no. 4 (October 1997): 289.

inspire us to work harder toward our goals. Watch someone who was born with no limbs, yet lives and works independently. Not only does he survive, but he uses those negative circumstances to spring forward and inspire others.

Before coaches can help others overcome the perils of the past, they need to look in the mirror. Why don't you turn your mess into your message? Your trials can actually become your story of triumph. You have the power to make that choice!

The Forward-Focused Coaching Model shifts attention from the problem to the solution to expedite the change process. Little or no attention is given to the past, diagnosis, history, or information gathering through this model. Attention is given primarily to the present and the future. To reinforce exception behavior of the past, coaches use EARS with their friends or clients. EARS is an acronym that invites coaches to elicit, amplify, reinforce, and start again.[22]

- Elicit—promote dialogue about exception behavior and positive thoughts
- Amplify—amplify and expand positive discoveries
- Reinforce—celebrate wins (large and small); tie to goals
- Start again—elicit more exception behavior and positives

To jumpstart someone's sense of hope for the future, the Miracle Question moves them from wondering "if" the dream will ever come true to considering the impact "when" it occurs. It envisions the person waking up the next day without the problem and asking what changes would take place. It pushes the person to imagine the specific, tangible, real improvement that would happen in day-to-day life. For example,

---

22 Fleming and Rickord, 289-290.

you might ask, "If you had all the resources you need right now, what steps would you take to fulfill your dream?"

Coaches who use Forward-Focused Coaching help people recall times when the problem is or has been less severe, or possibly even nonexistent. This reflection encourages them to describe what they did differently during those times, and it sets the goal for them to repeat the actions to achieve more positive results today.

Refuse to criticize, condemn, or complain. Instead, think and talk only about the things you really want.
—BRIAN TRACY

For example, you might ask someone who is weighed down by continual conflict at home or at work, "When have you responded with strength, kindness, and clarity in a conflict? What was going on in your life at that point that gave you a positive perspective and the courage to face difficult people?"

Scaling questions are used as tools to identify observable differences. These questions provide insight about the relative severity of the problem, and often give the person a fresh sense of hope to set and reach goals. In pain management, doctors often ask patients to pinpoint the current hurt on a scale of 1 (little or no pain at all) to 10 (excruciating, unbearable pain). The answer gives the doctor and the patient information about the patient's condition, especially in relation to previous indications of the pain.

For instance, a patient may say his pain from knee replacement surgery is a five. That's bad, but it's much better than the eight he endured last week.

In coaching, you might ask, "On a scale of 1 to 10, how would you rate your frustration with your boss? How would you have rated your frustration a year ago? On a scale of 1 to 10, how determined are you to achieve this goal?"

By showing genuine concern and admiration for the person's predicament or opportunity, the coach highlights the strengths of the person and focuses on his or her current coping skills. Coping sequence questions encourage people to appreciate the strengths they are using in the midst of the challenge.

A coach might observe, "I understand that things have been extremely difficult for you, yet you still manage to get up every day and face every difficulty. You're making real progress!" The coach then asks the person a question to uncover the coping skill he or she is using to manage the issue. This enables the one we're coaching to see specific strides he or she is making.

It's a big encouragement to have someone believe in us when we're under stress! When people trust us with their lives, we have a sacred privilege and responsibility to instill them with hope. Hope isn't ancillary. It isn't an add-on to their lives. It's absolutely essential. Without hope, they can't make progress toward their goals, and they won't stay strong when they face obstacles.

For example, consider the common issue of weight loss. If you're coaching someone who has tried several diets, counseling, and/or even surgery to assist in weight loss, but the person has repeatedly failed, hopelessness probably clouds your friend or client's mind and heart.

Frustrated people need to know there is still hope for them to succeed. Repeated failure is deeply discouraging, but now they've turned to you as a source of help and hope. This is a golden opportunity to put your coaching skills to work to help people succeed in weight loss. The answer, of course, is already inside them. Hope isn't found through a pill, a doctor, or a diet of seaweed and grapefruit. Those may contribute, but they are secondary solutions.

Losing weight won't be achieved overnight. Gaining the weight took time, and it will take time, energy, and effort to lose it. People experience true hope when you help them realize that being healthy is an obtainable goal. As a coach, you have the power to empower them!

CHAPTER 10

FACILITATING CHANGE

CASE STUDY

don't know what's wrong with me," complained Vicky as she had coffee with Jennifer. "I'm a competent person at work, but when it comes to relating to my family, I go numb . . . brain dead . . . incapable of even thinking coherent thoughts."

Jennifer has respected and admired Vicky as long as she's known her, but she noticed that this one area of her life created a reaction unlike any other. Vicky could analyze complex engineering problems and find creative solutions, and she enjoyed planning trips with Jennifer and a couple of other friends. In these activities, she was engaged, thoughtful, relaxed, and excited about the future.

Over time, Vicky shared more of her traumatic experiences with her father, and she explained that her mother hadn't protected her. She felt abused by one and abandoned by the other. Every time she thought about going back home for Christmas or any other event, her brain turned to mush. "In the days before I get on the plane, I can feel myself regressing back into childhood, and by the time I open the door to their house, I'm a terrified six year old. There's got to be a better way to live, but I feel stuck in the past."

Research has shown that the brains of many people are wired to stop rational thinking. An event, a challenging statement, or a facial expression causes an "amygdala hijacking," and a flood of powerful emotions effectively overwhelm the executive function of reasoning in the prefrontal cortex. When this happens, the person is driven to react, not think, and to try to cope with the moment by one of three defenses: fight, flight, or freeze. In the heat of the moment when we desperately need to think clearly, we simply can't. An article in the *Harvard Business Review* explains:

> *When we perceive a threat, the amygdala sounds an alarm, releasing a cascade of chemicals in the body. Stress hormones like adrenaline and cortisol flood our system, immediately preparing us for fight or flight. When this deeply instinctive function takes over, we call it what Daniel Goleman coined in* Emotional Intelligence *as "amygdala hijack." In common psychological parlance we say, "We've been triggered." We notice immediate changes like an increased heart rate or sweaty palms. Our breathing becomes more shallow and rapid as we take in more oxygen, preparing to bolt if we have to.*
>
> *The active amygdala also immediately shuts down the neural pathway to our prefrontal cortex, so we can become disoriented in a heated conversation. Complex decision-making disappears,*

as does our access to multiple perspectives. As our attention narrows, we find ourselves trapped in the one perspective that makes us feel the most safe: "I'm right and you're wrong," even though we ordinarily see more perspectives.[23]

Many of our friends or clients may not have full-blown amygdala hijackings as we talk to them, but we may notice particular points of resistance and the tendency to fight back, run away from problems (and us!), or become emotionally paralyzed. Change is still possible, but it requires coaches to be aware of these unhelpful reactions and provide a safe, supportive environment, so people can think more clearly and envision genuine change in their choices.

Your life does not get better by
chance, it gets better by change.
—JIM ROHN

The chart on the following page provides a graphic depiction of the process of change. At some point, people must carefully analyze the benefits and costs of change and determine if they are willing to pay the price to move forward.

---

23 Diane Musho Hamilton. "Calming Your Brain During Conflict," Harvard Business Review, December 22, 2015, https://hbr.org/2015/12/calming-your-brain-during-conflict.

STAGE 1
LOSS OF SECURITY

Feelings of:
FEAR

Thoughts of:
CAUTION

Behavior is:
CRIPPLING

STAGE 2
SELF-DOUBT

Feelings of:
RESISTANCE

Thoughts of:
UNBELIEF

Behavior is:
ANTAGONIZING

CHANGE

STAGE 6
CALL TO ACTION

Feelings of:
SUCCESS

Thoughts of: FOCUS

Behavior is:
EXUBERATING

RESPONSE TO CHANGE

STAGE 3
LOSS OF COMFORT

Feelings of:
ANTICIPATION

Thoughts of: FRAGMENTATION

Behavior is:
CHALLENGING

PIVOT ZONE

STAGE 5
FULFILLING THE CALL

Feelings of:
COURAGE

Thoughts of:
POSITIVITY

Behavior is:
PRODUCTIVE

STAGE 4
FINDING NEW IDENTITY

Feelings of:
EXPECTANCY

Thoughts of:
PROGRESS

Behavior is:
ENERGIZED

Curated from https://changecycle.com/change-cycle

CHAPTER 11

STAGES OF CHANGE

Over a period of three decades, James O. Prochaska and his colleagues developed the six stages of change. In their article, "Stages of Change," Prochaska and John C. Norcross define the stages of precontemplation, contemplation, preparation, action, maintenance, and termination.[24]

■ In the *precontemplation stage*, there is little or no consideration by the individual for changing direction or behavior. In fact, change is viewed as "irrelevant, unwanted, not needed, or impossible to achieve."[25] Individuals can remain for an extended period of time in this stage until they experience a compelling reason to change: social pressure, aging, illness, personal concerns, human development, shifts in values, or other significant influences. The

24 James O. Prochaska and John C. Norcross, "Stages of Change," Psychotherapy 38 (Winter 2001): 443-446.
25 DiClemente, Addiction and Change, 26.

task is for Precontemplators to increase awareness of the need for change, increase concern about the current pattern of behavior, and envision the possibility of change.[26]

- *Contemplation* is an ambivalent and emotional stage of weighing risks, benefits, pros and cons, and processes, and then considering what change would look like. The task in this stage is for Contemplators to resolve their "decisional balance considerations" in favor of change.[27]

- The decision to change marks the transition to the *preparation* stage. This stage involves making a commitment to change and creating a plan of action. The primary task for Preparers is to summon the courage and competencies to accomplish the change.[28]

- The *action* stage is the implementation stage of change. DiClemente recommends three to six weeks to establish a new pattern of behavior. The task for Actors is to continue to take steps forward over barriers and around challenges.[29]

- In the *maintenance* stage, the new behavior pattern becomes integrated into the individual's lifestyle, becomes automatic, and is the new status quo.[30]

- The final stage is *termination*. In some programs such as Alcoholics Anonymous, maintenance is the final stage of change because the person never stops the new behavior. However, in DiClemente's estimation, remaining in the maintenance stage has the "unwanted consequence of keeping the habit alive in some paradoxical manner."[31]

---

26 DiClemente, Addiction and Change, 26-27.
27 DiClemente, Addiction and Change, 28.
28 DiClemente, Addiction and Change, 28.
29 DiClemente, Addiction and Change, 29.
30 DiClemente, Addiction and Change, 29-30.
31 DiClemente, Addiction and Change, 201.

These stages are cyclical, at times difficult to categorize, and it is sometimes necessary to redo a stage until the task for each is thoroughly satisfied.

The process of change can be described in many different ways. The "Stairsteps to Transition" is much like "The Change Chart" in its flow and purpose, but some people find it more helpful. Consider the concept of stairsteps as a parallel to the previous chart. With your friends or clients, use the one that seems most helpful.

The Change Chart

DENYING THE NEED FOR CHANGE

RESISTING THE CHANGE

EXPLORING THE POSSIBILITIES

COMMITMENT TO TRANSITION

Denying the Need for Change:

(Remember, the first step of real progress is for people to realize how change will affect them.)

WHAT PEOPLE SAY	WHAT PEOPLE DO	WHAT THIS MEANS
"No big deal. Not sure what everyone is upset about."	Status Quo—work as usual	When people are in denial, they don't always grasp what they are told, they may not have actually heard what was said, or they don't absorb the information about the change. For this reason, they have not begun to figure out what the change means for them. They don't see the grand scheme of things.
"Heard it before; nothing ever changes."	No questions asked	
	No reaction	
"I'll believe it when I see it."	Show signs of:	
"Doesn't affect me."	• Apathy	
	• Shock	
"Nothing will change"	• Cooperation	
"What announce-ment? Oh, that, I didn't pay it much attention."	• Agreement	
	• Faith	
"No big deal. Done it before."		
"Oh, they are just going back to the old way of doing it."		

Resisting the Change:

At this step, people begin fearing how change may affect them.

WHAT PEOPLE SAY	WHAT PEOPLE DO	WHAT THIS MEANS
"Whose crazy idea was this anyway?"	Ask questions/ need details	Resistance happens whether people agree with change or not. The transition is what people resist, not necessarily the change. In other words, people are resisting the loss of what they know best, fearing the unknown, not the change itself. They feel they are losing identity and the way things are—the familiar—and they feel less competent.
"I wish things could just stay the same."	Complain/challenge	
"Why do they have to mess up a good thing?"	Point fingers/ blame others	
	Shoot down ideas	
"I feel so out of control. This will never work."	Become withdrawn	
	Have difficulty concentrating	
"How can they make a decision to change things they don't know any-thing about?"	Insomnia	
	When you don't deal with resistance you may see:	
"Now, wait a minute! What gives him or her the right to get in my lane?"	Increased incidents on the job	
	Sabotage of efforts	
"I don't have a problem with change; it's just *this* change."	Increased errors	
	Increased absences	
"I don't know how to do this."	Show signs of:	
"We've tried this before, and it didn't work, so why are we doing it again?"	• Self-absorption • Depression • Fear and/ or anger • Anxiety • Frustration • Distrust	

Exploring the Possibilities:

In this step, people attempt to understand what is happening and make appropriate and necessary adjustments.

WHAT PEOPLE SAY	WHAT PEOPLE DO	WHAT THIS MEANS
"We are so disorganized."	Make adjustments	Investigation of the change is a time of chaos and creativity that signals movement. This is the time between the old/status quo and the new/moving forward. It is a time when people are having feelings of being overwhelmed by the possibilities presented by the change and the work that still needs to be done to make the change effective.
"How did this come about? I forgot."	Make deals	
"I am so tired; I don't know which end is up."	Get involved	
"I can't sleep. I constantly wake up; my mind won't turn off."	Look for new rules and regulations	
"I'm so confused. One minute I'm confident and know what I'm doing; the next I feel so lost."	Brainstorm on ideas/options	
	Seek procedures, structure, and order	
"Wow, how scary! We could do anything; no one knows what anyone else is doing."	Show signs of: • Renewed optimism • Frustration • Confusion • Uncertainty • Excitement • Need for knowledge	
"We've got to get some organization here."		
"Where is our training? I don't know what I'm doing."		
"What is my job?"		
"Do we know the new procedures?"		

Commitment to Transition:

During this step, people settle in, adjust to new realities, and find ways to make change work.

WHAT PEOPLE SAY	WHAT PEOPLE DO	WHAT THIS MEANS
"I understand. I see what you mean."	Rebuild	True commitment to the change happens as people begin to make the necessary adjustments. Giving people the opportunity to express their concerns during the phases of resistance and exploration helps the commitment process. This is the point when change really begins and when you will find people are most ready, willing, and able to make it work.
"I finally am beginning to feel like myself again."	Cooperate	
"Our meetings are beginning to feel good."	Focus	
	Plan	
"This isn't so bad; I'm starting to get used to it."	Problem-solve	
	Make decisions	
"I can see ways to make this work."	Gain knowledge	
	Collaborate	
"I'm going to take a few courses to learn more."	Show signs of:	
	• Acceptance	
"Funny how upset we all got; it feels like it was forever ago."	• Satisfaction	
	• Confidence	
"This new job is OK."	• Teamwork	
	• Comfort	
"I'm sure they will change this too someday, but for now it feels like it will work."		
"It took me a while to get used to the team and learn how to work together, but now it feels like we have always worked together."		

People are different, and therefore, move through transition at different speeds with different needs at different times. Patience is necessary as well as remembering to monitor where people are in the process. As you coach people through change, you may become frustrated, feeling like they are unwilling to cooperate. It is more likely, though, that people are struggling with the challenges of transition instead of refusing to cooperate. Be observant, supportive, and attentive to the steps they are taking. When they are most vulnerable, they need your help even more.

Because people experience the steps of change with differing intensity and move through transition at differing speeds, you need to ask *yourself*:

- To what degree has this change taken them by surprise?
- To what degree does the change place them in an uncertain or unfamiliar situation?
- What is the size or quality of their loss?
- How does their age and stage of life affect their reaction?
- What other changes are they experiencing at the same time?
- What opportunities have they had to talk about their uncertainties?
- How does their personal style and degree of self-awareness affect their reaction?

Those who anticipate and plan for change will be ahead of the others affected by it. Some people thrive on the challenge of change, but many feel threatened. Be patient with those struggling to get on board with the change they are facing. Your support is critical to the success of their time of transition. Don't assume everyone will adopt the change, even if you give them plenty of time and encouragement. Actually, some will only adopt a change after they see the majority of people in the organization have done so. There will also always be a small minority that adopt change only when faced with dire consequences of not complying. For those who are hesitant to embrace change, help them create an environment with others who provide insight, support, and stimulation.

A clear vision of the future is compelling to some, but others are skeptical. Don't expect every person you coach to respond with eager enthusiasm. It's far more realistic to understand there are five different types of people, and each responds in their own way and pace. In *What's Shakin' Your Ladder*, Sam Chand identifies the five as:

1) **Excited Embracers . . .**
   - are excited to embrace our vision.
   - are ahead of the curve and believe that whatever we're proposing is a good idea the minute we suggest it.
   - don't need to hear all the details.
   - will feed off our vision, multiply it, and bring it back to us with new ideas.
   - have energy and are on top of things.

   Excited Embracers make up approximately only 2% of the population.

2) **Early Embracers . . .**
   - will embrace our vision early.
   - will stick with us as we work to make the vision a reality.

   Early Embracers make up approximately 18% of the population.

3) **Middlers . . .**

- hear our vision and want more time to think about it.
- are not against the vision, but neither are they for it.
- won't make up their minds one way or another unless a friend convinces them to.

Middlers make up 60% of the population.

4) **Late Embracers . . .**

- have already decided that they aren't in favor of whatever is on the table.
- might grudgingly follow when they see there are no other choices.

They make up approximately 18% of the population.

5) **Never Embracers . . .**

- disagree, no matter what the subject is.
- have their minds already set.

Fortunately, they make up only 2% of the population.

As we get ready to cast the vision, we need to target the Middlers, the 60% who have not yet made up their minds.

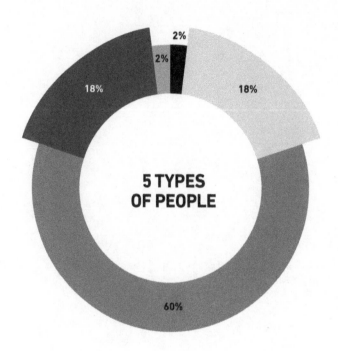

2%

2%

18%

18%

5 TYPES OF PEOPLE

60%

Excited Embracers

Early Embracers

Middlers

Late Embracers

Never Embracers

PART 3

The Practice of Coaching

CHAPTER 12

THE IMPORTANCE OF SELF-DISCOVERY

CASE STUDY

Suzanne and Mary Jo had been friends for years. They moved into houses only a couple of doors away from each other, and since then, they've juggled the responsibilities of raising their children, encouraging their husbands, and working in the corporate world. For the past six months, Mary Jo has been feeling a lot of pressure to spend more time with her three grade-school children. She has talked with Suzanne a number of times about her dilemma, but she hasn't come to a decision about what course to take.

In their most recent conversation, it was obvious that Mary Jo had hit a wall. Soon after she and Suzanne sat down at the coffee shop, she blurted out, "I'm so confused. I can't make a decision. Suzanne, just tell me what to do!"

Suzanne could have easily said, "Let me get out a sheet of paper and list out the pros and cons of your choices," but she didn't. She resisted the temptation to take control and give "the right answer." Instead, she asked questions to get below the surface and help her friend discover some insights about herself. She asked, "Does this situation remind you of times in the past when you've felt stuck and couldn't make a decision?"

Mary Jo thought for a few seconds, and then her eyes lit up. "Yeah! Come to think of it. This has happened every time I've had to make hard choices."

Susanne asked her to tell about some of them, and Mary Jo quickly connected her current doubts and fears to times when she struggled in the past. After several stories, Suzanne asked, "What do you think is the insight about yourself that's beneath your reluctance to make these decisions?"

This led to a number of conversations in the days that followed. Mary Jo gained much more understanding of herself and the way her fears had clouded her thoughts for many years . . . and Suzanne avoided taking the dumb risk of trying to come up with "the right answer" which easily could have backfired.

One of the foundational principles of coaching is that the person being coached sets goals and takes steps to execute them. Coaches aren't counselors, mentors, consultants, or parents to their friends or clients! Results are more effective when people make decisions about the specific behaviors they want to control or change. In self-management programs, the coach's role is to help others process their behavior modification. To accomplish this, the coach must be authentic in the relationship, so others can increasingly lead self-directed lives and avoid being dependent on experts to deal with their problems.[32] Individuals are encouraged to accept the responsibility for carrying out self-management strategies in everyday life. Some self-management strategies include self-monitoring, self-reward, self-contracting, stimulus control, and self-as-model.[33]

Cormier and Nurius have identified five essential characteristics for an effective self-management program:

1) A combination of self-management strategies is usually more useful than a single strategy.

2) Self-management efforts need to be employed regularly over a sustained period, or their effectiveness may be too limited to produce any significant change.

3) It is essential that people make a self-evaluation and set goals that are personally meaningful to them.

4) The use of self-reinforcement is an important component of self-management programs.

5) Some degree of environmental support is necessary to maintain changes that result from a self-management program.[34]

A man can never hope to be more than he is
if he is not first honest about what he isn't.

—DON WILLIAMS JR.

---

32 Corey, Theory and Practice of Counseling and Psychotherapy, 248.
33 Corey, 248.
34 S. Cormier, and P. S. Nurius, Interviewing and Change Strategies for Helpers: Fundamental Skills and Cognitive Behavioral Interventions, 5th ed. (Pacific Grove, CA: Brooks/Cole, 2003), 586-589, quoted in Gerald Corey, Theory and Practice of Counseling and Psychotherapy, 7th ed. (Belmont, CA: Brooks/Cole-Thomson Learning, 2005), 249.

Additionally, Watson and Tharp offer five basic steps that must be followed in a self-management program to effect change:

1) Selecting goals.

2) Translating goals into target behaviors.

3) Self-monitoring (which involves the individual observing his or her own behavior—including cues and consequences).

4) Working out an action plan (includes methods such as punishment, stimulus control, behavioral contracts, and social support).

5) Evaluating an action plan for necessary adjustments.[35]

Self-directed behavior is an essential tool in coaching. Rather than looking to a counselor or someone else to tell someone what to do, the person discovers the answers himself. *This is the key to successful coaching.* As a coach, there is no more fulfilling moment than when we see someone have an "aha!" moment.

When the light bulb is turned on in their mind, and we see it in their countenance, we know they've found the answer that was inside them all along. This is when we know we're fulfilling our role as coaches.

There is nothing noble in being superior
to your fellow man; true nobility is
being superior to your former self.
—ERNEST HEMINGWAY

---

35 D. L. Watson and R. G. Tharp, *Self-directed Behavior: Self-modification for Personal Adjustment*, 8th ed. (Pacific Grove, CA: Brooks/Cole, 2002), quoted in Gerald Corey, *Theory and Practice of Counseling and Psychotherapy*, 7th ed. (Belmont, CA: Brooks/Cole—Thomson Learning, 2005), 249-250.

CHAPTER 13

ACTIVE LISTENING

CASE STUDY

Phil came home from work exhausted mentally and physically. As usual, he came through the door and was met by his five-year-old daughter, Alicia. She hugged his leg, and he patted her on the head. He went to the kitchen and got a glass of water, and he slumped on the sofa. Like he always did, he turned on the news while Alicia tried to tell him all about her day: her doll's new dress, the dog catching a squirrel, and her tea party with her imaginary friends. And like he always did, Phil barely took his eyes off the television. Alicia climbed up on the arm of the sofa, took her father's face in her hands, and turned his gaze toward her. She said, "I'm over here, Dad. I'm over here. If you're not looking at me, I don't think you hear anything I say."

When people want us to listen, we can be distracted like Phil, or we can be preoccupied with planning our reply to the person talking to us. Robert Montgomery once asked, "Are you really listening . . . or are you just waiting for your turn to talk?"

Communication is a two-way street of speaking and listening. Listening is a vital element of communication, but it is often underestimated or even ignored. Even though more waking hours are spent listening than any other activity, few people are good listeners. We are often taught how to improve our speaking skills, but rarely are we taught to listen more effectively. Active listening is a habit, and it is the foundation of effective communication. Coaches need to understand and practice these skills.

Hearing and listening are often considered one and the same. However, they are categorically different. We hear sounds, but often we hear them without really listening to them.

HEARING

- Physical act of receiving sounds
- Passive act - it happens even in our sleep

LISTENING

- Active Process - requires work
- Not only hearing - but paying attention, understand and assimilate what is heard
- Involves interaction

The words people say only constitute 7% of the total communication. Fifty-five percent of meaning is expressed in body language, and 38% through the tone of voice. This is one reason online conversations, text messages, and emails are so difficult to decipher.

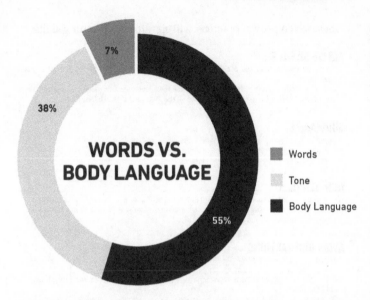

In the process of listening, we should be so focused on the person and the message that we can repeat what the speaker has said—so accurately, in fact, that the speaker will say, "That's it! You understand me!" This is not to say you necessarily agree with the speaker, but rather, you understand what he or she is saying—both the content and the feelings.

The process of listening can be learned, and in fact, it is an acquired skill for all of us. Learning to listen is only achieved by sustained and conscious effort. The more you try to listen, the more you'll understand. You choose to listen or not to listen; you control the process.

These seven proven practices will elevate your listening skills:

ACTIVE SILENCE
- When you are listening, speak only when you need clarification or to summarize what you have heard.
- Do not be afraid of the silence—by allowing silence in your conversation, you may actually get more information than if you jump in to fill the awkwardness of silence.

SUMMARIZE
- Summarize, in your own words, what the client has told you.
- This allows you to make sure you have understood everything correctly
- It lets your client know you truly are listening.

NON-VERBALS
- How you present yourself to your client determines what or how much they will tell you.
- If your non-verbals relay the message that you are uninterested, bored, or in a hurry, your client will be less likely to engage with you.

AVOID DISTRACTIONS
- Imagine you are telling someone about the biggest crisis of your life. Just when you are about to get to the main point, the phone rings and your listener takes the call
- Even if the topic is not extremely personal or emotional, people want to know they have your full attention.
- By closing your office door or silencing your phone and not taking calls, you have let your client know that she is your main focus.

CLEAR YOUR HEAD
- You should free your mind of your own problems and concerns when listening to others.
- Push back any preconceived ideas you may have about the person or topic.
- Keep an open mind.

STAY AWAY
- Listening—unlike hearing—is an active job.
- If you are so tired you are nodding off, or if you are preoccupied with something, you might suggest setting up an alternative time to talk to avoid offending or hurting your speaker.

STAY CALM
- If your speaker Is using highly emotional words or getting visibly upset, remain calm.
- If you allow yourself to become over-stimulated by what is being said, you will not be able to focus on the main point.
- If you encounter a "talker" and need to keep it short, let them know right from the start that you only have fifteen minutes (or whatever your time limit may be). If you make this clear, there should be no hurt feelings when you get ready to leave after fifteen minutes.
- Establish together your goal of the conversation and continually refer to it. For example, you may decide at the beginning of your meeting that your goal is to figure out how to improve member participation at your organization's meetings. Whenever your client gets off track, you could say, "How does this relate to member participation at meetings?" or "That's really interesting and I'd love to hear about it later, but for the moment we need to stick to our goal."

In an article for Korn Ferry, Gary Burnison remarked, "Listening is to hearing as observing is to seeing. Listening and observing are participative—we're all in and we're fully present."[36] We sometimes refer to a presenter as "an eloquent speaker." We mean that the communication is clear, insightful, and compelling. We could also describe some coaches as "eloquent listeners" because they invite the other person to be transparent, self-reflective, and thorough.

---

36 Gary Burnison, "Are We Listening?" KornFerry, February 28, 2021.

CHAPTER 14

MOTIVATIONAL INTERVIEWING

When Sam Chand came from India as a student, he spent his first night in the United States in a dorm room. In the middle of the night, the roar of a train passing only a few feet behind the dorm startled him! After a couple of weeks, however, he got used to the noise of the nightly train and slept soundly through the night. He became conditioned to his new environment, so he didn't even notice the trains any longer.

The same phenomenon happens to all of us. We become so familiar with the noise of life that we don't even notice it any longer: chaos has become normal. At different points, we need to step back and make a courageous, honest appraisal of our lives. When we become acutely aware of our past, present, and future, we can make a concerted effort to "do life" intentionally!

Motivational interviewing is an important coaching technique. This approach is collaborative (it honors the participant's expertise and perspective) and evocative (it assumes that resources and motivation for change reside within the friend or client; perceptions, goals and values are drawn from the participant), and it promotes autonomy (the participant's right and capacity for self-direction are affirmed and facilitated).[37] There are four general principles in motivational interviewing:

1) *Express empathy* (acceptance facilitates change).

2) *Support self-efficacy* (others are responsible for choosing and carrying out change; coach's belief in the person's ability to change becomes a self-fulfilling prophecy, participant presents the arguments for change).

3) *Roll with resistance* (avoid arguing for change, the friend or client is the primary resource in finding answers and solutions; resistance is a signal to respond differently).

4) *Develop discrepancy* (change is motivated by perceived discrepancy between present behavior and important personal goals or values).[38]

When you practice these techniques with others, these practices will change you as well. If you act like you believe in people, soon you'll find yourself actually instinctively believing in them more than you ever thought possible. That's how disciplines work! You change the way you act, and ultimately, the way you think and feel changes with it. When you listen intently, ask great questions, and keep people accountable,

---

37 William R. Miller and Stephen Rollnick, Motivational Interviewing: Preparing People for Change, 2nd ed., (New York, NY: The Guilford Press, 2002), 35.
38 Miller and Rollnick, 36-41.

you are telling them you believe in them, and you are growing in your capacity as a coach.

Rigorous reflection can be a challenge, but when we see patterns of strength and fulfillment taking shape as we look at our past, we often have a renewed and refined sense of direction for the future. Convergence is trending toward a common result as different streams of experiences, relationships, and preferences flow together guiding our conscious and unconscious decisions.

It is the nature, and the advantage, of strong people that they can bring out the crucial questions and form a clear opinion about them. The weak always have to decide between alternatives that are not their own.

—DIETRICH BONHOEFFER

As we explored in Part 2, outside factors may force change on people, but coaching is designed to facilitate self-initiated, self-directed change. Our goal isn't to make people alter their lives, but to help them take the steps they want to take. In self-management programs, the coach's role is to guide the process. This involves the coach being willing to share his or her knowledge so that people can increasingly lead self-directed lives and not be dependent on the coach (or other experts) to deal with their problems. The coach's role is to help clarify the person's goals, sharpen the plans, encourage each step forward, and teach coping skills to deal with the inevitable difficulties in the process.

As we've seen, hope is the fuel of growth. Many coaches and other professionals have used the key principles found in C. R. Snyder's *Handbook of Hope*. Snyder's hope-building process is comprised of two stages. The first stage is instilling hope through "hope finding and hope bonding," and the second stage is increasing hope through "hope enhancing and hope reminding."[39]

- *Hope finding* involves listening for strands of hope in the person's story and identifying hope-filled themes—in other words, finding hope that already exists.

- *Hope bonding* involves developing a trusting relationship between coach and a friend or client, modeling hope through language and behavior, and the coach collaborating with the person to uncover components of hopeful thinking in his or her story.

- *Hope enhancing* involves identifying the strengths of the one we're coaching and encouraging optimistic thinking—not painting all things rosy, but finding a single positive aspect as a bedrock of optimism for the future.

- Finally, *hope reminding* is an intentional search to identify the person's previously successful endeavors.

These four elements of hope profoundly encourage people and build their sense of confidence. Many coaches instinctively do these things for others, but all of us can become more intentional and skilled in these approaches.

---

39 C. R. Snyder, Handbook of Hope: Theory, Measures, and Applications, (San Diego, CA: Academic Press, 2000), 127-146.

> When you stop learning, stop listening,
> stop looking and asking questions—always
> new questions—then it is time to die.
> **—LILLIAN SMITH**

In motivational interviews, each coaching session contains basic questions relating to the person's overall goal. People are held accountable for the personal goals they set. Due to the nature of coaching, sessions with each participant have an organic flow and are uniquely tailored. The people we coach have the freedom to set personal goals and agenda and be guided by their values.

Hope is the fuel of genuine and lasting change. As we saw in Part 1, the most effective way of helping people find hope is to ask a series of questions. Imagining possibilities, considering opportunities and options, and daring to see a better future will breed a fresh sense of confidence. The following questions (reemphasized below) are suggestions to consider using. We are never to assume how the questions will be answered because every person is unique.

- "Envision a life full of fulfilled dreams, and tell me how that looks. Don't hold back; this is your dream." (These types of questions allow people to get outside of their closed boxes ... to imagine if their pasts weren't holding them back what their lives would look like.)

- "What do you believe is stopping you from being able to realize those dreams?" (This presents the reality, the stress point, or the snag. There's nothing wrong with allowing those we coach to become angry or emotional when they realize how their past has controlled and robbed them. That's powerful fuel to promote change!)

■ "What will your life be like a few months from now if you don't make the decision to change the patterns of the past?" (This question presents the danger of remaining in bondage to the past.)

■ "When you consider your dream, do you see yourself as valuable and deserving of this dream? Why or why not?"

■ "Have you allowed something or someone to steal your sense of self-worth? If so, what will be different this time?"

The point of these questions is to help people identify the blockage caused by unresolved pain or personal failures from the past, and then to have them vividly imagine the future without that baggage. This propels them into hopeful thinking.

CHAPTER 15

USING PLANS

n coaching, acronyms are often used to remember concepts and tools. Acronyms use shortcuts in the English language and are valuable memory devices. A study conducted by Gerald R. Miller found that students who used mnemonic devices such as acronyms improved their test scores by up to 77%. Dream Releaser Coaching uses such universal acronyms as: SMART, GROW, ANTS, and PETS, to name a few. Coaches-in-training are encouraged to develop acronyms of their own as desired and/or needed as a memory device.

An essential acronym in coaching is one we developed using the word PLANS. We believe this incorporates the five most important components of any coaching session.

In order to be an effective coach, you must utilize PLANS:

Powerful Questions

Listening

Accountability

Neutrality

Silence (is your best friend.)[40]

Powerful questions are stimulating inquiries that cut through evasion and confusion. By asking powerful questions, the person is then able to reach points of clarity, action, and discovery at a whole new level. These are often questions that most people tend to avoid asking themselves. It allows him or her to dive deep into evaluating their situation and begin to form their plan to achieve their desired result.

Powerful questions evoke discovery and insight during motivational interviews, and simultaneously demonstrate that the coach is actively listening and understanding what is being conveyed by the one we're coaching.

An example of a powerful question may be:

- "What risk would you take if you knew you could not fail?"
- "What is standing in your way of moving forward in achieving this goal?"
- "Now that you've identified your obstacles, what steps will you take to overcome them?"
- "What does your life look like in two years if you don't make this transition? What does it look like if you DO make this transition?"

Listening actively is something you consciously choose to do while hearing is simply the act of perceiving sound by the ear. Hearing simply happens while listening requires concentration. Listening is intentional

---

40 The PLANS concept was developed by DRC's Executive Director, Dr. Christopher Bowen. Used by permission.

and is one of the most important skills in coaching. How well you listen has a major impact on your effectiveness as a coach.

We not only listen to gather information; we listen to understand and learn. It builds the intimacy and trust with the person, which is an essential component of the core competencies of the International Coaching Federation. Genuine listening results in less wasted time and more forward-focused, purposeful coaching.

Be sure to pay attention to not just what is said but to nonverbal cues as well. Face the speaker, maintain eye contact, and be present and attentive. As we have more online video appointments, we need to pay even more attention to the subtle hints of gestures, facial expressions, and voice inflections.

Accountability is essential in coaching as it requires the person we're coaching to take ownership and accept responsibility for moving toward their goals.

The International Coaching Federation defines managing progress and accountability as the "ability to hold attention on what is important for the client, and to leave responsibility with the client to take action."[41]

While it is NOT the responsibility or privilege of the coach to promote their own requirements or suggestions, accountability can be demonstrated by asking the person about their action steps set in previous sessions and acknowledging people for what they have or have not done. Accountability allows the person to stay on track toward the big picture of where they're heading and keeps them open to adjustments that may need to be made to continue their progress.

---

41 https://coachfederation.org/core-competencies.

Neutrality is sometimes a challenge for coaches. Coaching is other-led with the responsibility and credit for change remaining with the person, not the coach. Coaching helps people discover for themselves what is necessary to achieve their goals. The most sensible knowledge a coach should exhibit is that of the coaching process itself, which empowers the person to facilitate their own way forward.

As much as we are engaged in wanting to see the person obtain good results, the moment the coach is convinced that they know "the right way" for someone is the moment they have robbed the person from sustaining long-term personal development. Coaching isn't an opportunity to demonstrate the coach's in-depth knowledge but rather to promote the person's own knowledge and discoveries of what will work in their own lives.

A coach offering his or her own opinion or recommendation is leading and guiding the friend or client's action and conduct. Coaches are privileged to help others open their own minds, consider their own options, and discover their own potential.

Silence is your best friend! While exercising silence in coaching can sometimes feel as if you've run out of powerful questions, silence is a powerful coaching skill in confirming your ability to really listen to your friend or client. Silence reminds you, as a coach, to not impose your solution, but rather to allow the person the space they need to detect their own.

Silence allows people the time to consider the powerful question you have just presented to them. It also allows them to think through their answer and to consider exploring further options, or setting action to the ones they've realized.

As awkward as silence can sometimes feel, don't rush to rob the one you're coaching of the time to think for themselves. They are wishing to explore and reflect; silence allows this opportunity. Take the time to pause, allowing the person to pursue their own reactions and allowing the coach to be sure they have provided this opportunity. As Will Rogers said, "Never miss a good chance to shut up."

CHAPTER 16

SETTING SMART GOALS

As coaches, perhaps the most common request we hear is to help others set clearer goals . . . and help them create the tracks to reach them. Goals aren't optional. Without a compelling sense of purpose, people lose their reason to live. Without a vision of a meaningful future, relationships become stale, conversation is empty, and every day becomes an endless grind. No matter what a person's religion or creed, we all have an instinctive sense that we were put on earth for a reason. Our task as coaches is first to uncover and live out our own destiny, and then to help those we coach find and fulfill theirs. No one can fulfill another's purpose in life; each of us is responsible for our own. What paths we take, what roads we go, and how we reach that end are all determined by our choices.

> The greater danger for most of us is not
> that our aim is too high and we miss it,
> but that it is too low and we hit it.
> —**MICHELANGELO BUONARROTI, RENAISSANCE ARTIST**

The path to a desired destiny is a sequence of opportunities—sometimes disguised as colossal problems. What we do with those—which ones we grab, which ones we pass, what we endure, or where we fail—is entirely up to each of us.

The opportunities and challenges we encounter are like paths and barriers on an open field. We can take an easy path or blaze a new trail. We can halt at a barrier, jump over it, or find a new path. The obstacles, though, don't determine our destination; our choices do. In effect, we have absolute control of our choices. Victor Frankl, a psychiatrist who survived the Nazi death camps, reflected, "Everything can be taken from a man or a woman but one thing: the last of human freedoms—to choose one's attitude in any given set of circumstances, to choose one's own way."

In his book, *Attitude is Everything,* Paul J. Meyer describes the characteristics of S.M.A.R.T. goals. (This term first surfaced in the November 1981 issue of *Management Review* by George T. Doran.) This graphic provides descriptive words for each element of these goals.

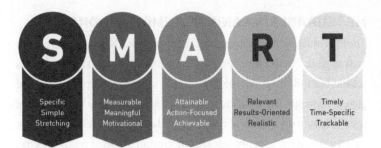

SPECIFIC/SIMPLE/STRETCHING

Goals should be specific, simple, and stretching. This means the goal is clear and unambiguous, and it should stretch the person's mind and heart with a bigger vision of the future. Some people resort to clichés to avoid thinking too deeply. Specific goals allow the person to know exactly *what* is expected, *why* it is important, *who's* involved, *where* it is going to happen, and *which* attributes are important.

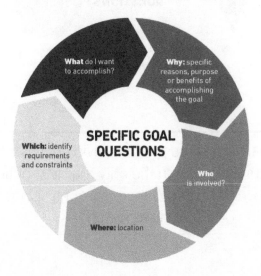

MEASURABLE/MEANINGFUL/MOTIVATIONAL

The goal must be measurable, meaningful, and motivational. The person setting goals needs clear criteria for measuring progress and a sound reason behind the goal. The goal should motivate the person toward genuine change. The ability to measure progress will help the one you're coaching stay on track and reach target dates. A compelling meaning underpinning the goal provides the motivational fuel to reach the goal.

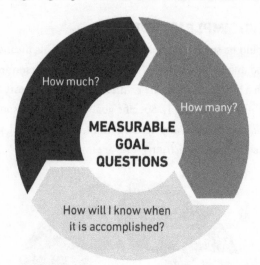

Learn from the past, set vivid goals for the
future, and live in the only moment of time
over which you have any control: now.
—DENIS WAITLEY

ATTAINABLE/ACTION-FOCUSED/ACHIEVABLE

The goal should be attainable, action-focused, and achievable. Good goals should stretch people, but not to the breaking point. People need to see "small wins," so they stay motivated. To make progress, the goals need to focus on specific steps the person can take—not broad, general concepts.

All goals aren't of equal importance. By identifying goals that are most important to people, the coach can remain focused on the priorities in others' lives. The friends or clients, too, focus on their priorities and avoid getting distracted by secondary hopes and problems. In this way, people develop attitudes, abilities, skills, and financial capacity to reach their goals. When one set of goals is reached, the coach and friend or client may then identify the next goals to tackle.

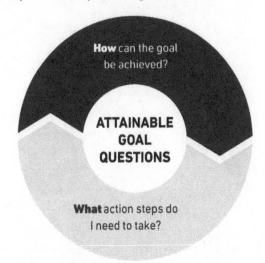

> Too many of us are not living our dreams
> because we are living our fears.
> —**LES BROWN**

RELEVANT/RESULTS-ORIENTED/REALISTIC

Goals that don't inspire or challenge quickly become irrelevant to people. For example, a bank manager may set a goal to "make fifty peanut butter and jelly sandwiches by 2:00 pm." This goal is specific, measurable, attainable, and time-bound, but it desperately lacks relevance! Relevant goals drive the person forward by providing continued motivation.

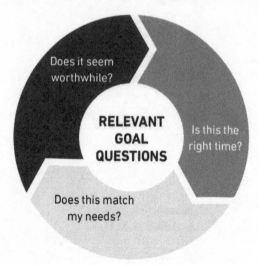

TIMELY/TIME-SPECIFIC/TRACKABLE

Goals must be grounded in a specific time frame. Target dates keep people focused and enable coaches to hold them accountable. Without deadlines, other priorities can easily rearrange their daily list of things to do, crowding out the top goals he or she has set. A time-bound goal is intended to establish a sense of urgency.

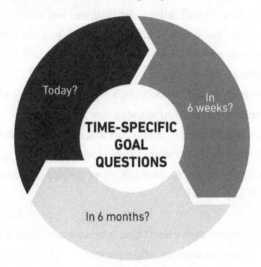

The difference between a fantasy and a goal is that we don't really anticipate achieving a fantasy. Goals are concrete things. To achieve them, we take bold, clear, achievable, intentional steps.

Without a goal, we are just fantasizing about our desires, but we're not making any progress toward genuine progress. There's nothing wrong with being a dreamer. In fact, it's sad when people are too afraid to dream. But dreams have to take shape, and specific goals give them shape and substance.

Goals are the yardstick of life. We set goals to accomplish specific steps of progress, and we may need to set short-term and intermediate goals to fulfill our long-term goals. Goal setting is both art and science. We develop the skill with lots of practice. Some people are naturally gifted in establishing clear benchmarks of progress, but most people need some help to clarify the destination and the path to get there.

If you're new to goal setting, get your feet wet with a few, small, personal goals. "Small wins" will keep you motivated and provide clear direction for larger goals.

Examples of "small wins":

- Sending out appreciation cards to people who matter to you.
- Drinking one less can of soda a day.
- Finally getting your credit report to see where your credit stands.
- Making sure to tell your kids you love them at least once a day.
- Taking your lunch instead of going through the drive-thru at least once a week.

Setting personal goals doesn't have to be a big deal. Start small; make progress. It's getting started that's important.

It's important for a friend or client (or a coach) to set goals that really matter. If a goal doesn't capture our hearts, it will end up in the trash can—and pretty quickly. Solid goals should make a difference in our sense of purpose, our vision for the future, and our most important relationships.

When you're 100% certain, you're too late.
—CHARLES W. ROBINSON

COMMON MISTAKES

Many people have difficulty setting goals, and even more struggle to achieve the ones they've articulated. Here are some common mistakes people make:

■ Setting unrealistic goals

The most common mistake made in setting goals is setting the bar too high. When we expect too much from ourselves or from others, the most likely outcome will be disappointment. We need to "keep it real."

■ Focusing on too few areas

We need to be able to see the "big picture." Yes, we need to focus on short-term goals, but if we have no view of where we ultimately want to go, we have little motivation to make the small goals become reality.

■ Underestimating the time it will take to accomplish a goal

Expecting too much too fast sets us up for disappointment. It's like saying you'll build a house from the ground up in a few weeks. You have to keep expectations realistic and make room for the unexpected.

■ Being devastated by failure

Most people don't realize that failure can be one of the most positive forces in our lives. It can motivate us to be more creative instead of causing us to give up in frustration. A famous inventor once said he didn't fail a thousand times before he succeeded. He'd only found a thousand ways it didn't work first!

■ Setting "other people's goals" instead of our own

We need to respect the boundaries of other people—especially those we love and those we work with each day. We have our dreams; they have theirs. We have our goals; they have their own. We can become partners, but only if we work hard to have compatible visions of the future. We can't allow ourselves to try to live someone else's dreams. We can be inspired by others, and we can inspire them, but each person has to own his own destiny, purpose, and goals.

■ Not reviewing progress

It's important to move our focus off past frustrations and achievements, but we need to learn from the past. If it weren't for the small steps, we wouldn't appreciate our progress. Small steps, not huge leaps, get us to our destinies.

■ Setting "negative" goals

When we think negatively, we act negatively. We become obsessed with our failures, the people who have blocked our goals, and all we've lost in the process. Resentment poisons the hearts of those who develop negative goals of "getting back" at those who hurt them.

■ Setting too many goals

The old phrase, "Keep it simple" is still good advice. If our "to-do" list is too large, we get frustrated and give up. We need to look at our list and prioritize what's most important, so we can avoid becoming overwhelmed.

DEALING WITH DISAPPOINTMENT

Everybody handles disappointment differently. Some feel sorry for themselves, some get mad, and others go into denial. The question is, "How do *you* handle disappointment?"

An article written by Barton Goldsmith, PhD, LMFT, published by *Psychology Today* states, "Feeling sorry for yourself only blocks you from achieving your goals"[42] and keeps you from moving forward. When faced with an obstacle or delay, ask yourself, *What's the worst that could happen?* You need to do something constructive because life is a limited

---

42 Barton Goldsmith, PhD, LMFT, "How to Deal with Disappointment," Psychology Today, June 20, 2011, https://www.psychologytoday.com/us/blog/emotional-fitness/201106/how-deal-disappointment.

window of opportunity, and you don't want to waste your time on what didn't work for you. A better alternative to self-pity is to seek out other opportunities or find a positive role model.

Channeling energy in a positive direction is a choice, not a feeling. Once you get started, you may soon find that your mood will lighten, you'll be able to focus on your goals, and you'll be more thankful (instead of sullen and grouchy).

Self-pity soon sours and turns into bitterness and resentment. Being mad at yourself or someone else, Goldsmith maintains, "weakens your emotional and physical immune system. All your energy goes into dealing with your anger, and you have few resources for anything else." In reality, no one gets everything they want. When you feel disappointment, getting mad or pouting is only going to make the situation and your feelings worse.

Instead of getting mad, choose to look at the blessings, benefits, and other things that make you smile. Take a walk. Go to a game or a museum. Do something fun and get your mind off your troubles. Things may not be moving as fast as you'd like, but maybe they are going at the right speed. If you force the situation, you may not like its outcome.

Sometimes we get upset with ourselves because we have unintentionally hurt someone we love, or perhaps we feel like an idiot because we did or said something stupid. If you've wronged someone, have the courage to admit it and ask for forgiveness. Don't blame, excuse, or deny the event and your part in it, and don't expect instant love, joy, and forgiveness. Give the person time to grieve, heal, and forgive you. It is best for everyone involved—even you!

Denial of reality—harm done to us or harm we've inflicted on others—stunts our emotional, spiritual, and relational growth. We need a safe, wise person who can help us process our pain and show us the path to love, peace, and reconciliation. Goldsmith warns that holding back your feelings is "the first ingredient in a recipe for disaster. Holding things in or ignoring them will only make you feel worse. Those around you will get the vibe and perhaps pull away," ultimately hurting you and them even more. Goldsmith finishes wisely, "So the next time you don't get what you want, remember that what you wanted may not have been what you really needed." Every pain or every setback is a classroom for us to learn life's biggest lessons.

CHAPTER 17

THE GROW MODEL

The G.R.O.W. model is an acronym that was developed in the United Kingdom by Sir John Whitmore; it is frequently used as a coaching tool. GROW stands for **G**oals, **R**eality, **O**ptions, and **W**ill.

This model enables the coach to structure effective coaching sessions. This model is powerful because it is easily understood, straightforward to apply, and thorough. It provides a structured process for goals and challenges, breaking down an issue into its constituent parts. Once these are clear, solutions can be developed more readily.

GOALS

- Ask the client to set an agenda for a coaching conversation.
- Evaluate the client's goal against the S.M.A.R.T. goal as the standard.
- Example: "I'd like to have three new alternatives to explore by the end of our time together."

REALITY

- This step defines the starting point, such as where things are at this moment.
- Ask for actual data, not impressions.
- The purpose of the reality check is to be as objective as possible about the current situation.
- Examples: "How much do you weigh now?" or "How many times in the last week did you go to the gym?"

OPTIONS

- Help your client explore possible solutions.
- At first, your client probably will be thinking inside the box. Help the client identify the box and look at the problem from a new angle.
- Simply try to get new alternatives on the table at this point without too much analysis.
- Examples: "What options have you considered?" or "What else could you try?"

WILL

- This is the action step.
- Help the client analyze the options that were generated and decide on a course of action.
- Anticipate obstacles that might come up.
- Talk about the kind of support structure necessary for the change to occur.

By the end of this process, people should be able to answer the following questions:

- "What will I do?"
- "When will I do it by?"
- "How will I meet the obstacles along the way?"
- "Who will provide support, encouragement, and/or accountability?"
- "Am I committed to this course of action?"

It is not always what we know or analyze before we make a decision that makes it a great decision. It is what we do after we make the decision to implement and execute it that makes it a good decision.

**—WILLIAM POLLARD,
CHAIRMAN OF THE SERVICEMASTER COMPANY**

CHAPTER 18

OVERCOMING BARRIERS

CASE STUDY

Laura graduated from college and got a job with a marketing firm, but her heart had always been in caring for people. To her boss's surprise, she announced that she had applied to nursing school, and she'd been accepted. When the next semester began, she was in her element in her classes. Sarah excelled in school and got a great job working for a local hospital. After a couple of years, her vision expanded, and she decided to apply for a slot to train as a physician's assistant. It would mean more training, more responsibility, and better pay.

She applied to two medical schools with PA programs. One turned her down, but she was one of one hundred applicants who were invited to interview at the other school. She studied hard and got input from others in the program. When she walked into the interview, she was ready. The interview went well, and she was surprised a few weeks later when she got the letter that she hadn't been accepted. She wasn't only surprised; she was devastated. It was the death of a dream . . . or was it?

Sarah worked hard as a nurse and kept studying in her off hours, and she applied again to the two schools. Like déjà vu, she was turned down by one and made the first cut for the second one. This time, she was even more prepared for the interview, but again, she wasn't accepted.

She told her best friend, "I don't know if this is the end or not. I surely want to be a PA, but it doesn't look like I'm cut out for it." Again, Sarah had to decide if the wall was the end of the line or an obstacle to climb over.

A *barrier* is a physical structure which blocks or obstructs a person from reaching a desired destiny. In order to develop a successful strategy for change for those you coach, you need to understand the types of barriers they face as they try to reach their personal goals, and ultimately, their destiny. With this knowledge, they can consider which barriers are most problematic and prioritize them. You can then help them identify relevant solutions. By following this lesson carefully, you can develop a tailored approach to overcome the barriers in the lives of your friends or clients (and in your own life), encourage changes in behavior, and achieve desired goals.

Everything can be taken from a man or a woman but one thing: the last of human freedoms to choose one's attitude in any given set of circumstances, to choose one's own way.

—VICTOR FRANKL

The goal of the coach is to assist the person in reaching his or her destiny, and this is often a challenging task because significant barriers may hold them back from achieving their dreams. In order to make progress on the journey to success, it's necessary to identify and remove these barriers. The first step in dealing with them is to give them a name and realize the role they play in blocking progress. Then we can help people remove these barriers one by one and get them closer to each goal.

External Barriers	Internal Barriers
Overcoming Barriers	Habits
Excessive demands	Fear and Insecurity
Difficult people	Negative mindset
Criticism	Noncommittal / no ownership or responsibility
Unclear boundaries	Resistance to change
No evaluation from others	Impatience / boredom
Energy drainers	Goals change

Barriers come in many shapes and sizes. Some are external and visible, but many are internal attitudes, beliefs, and fears. Sometimes barriers can be very easy to identify. For instance, a person you're coaching may dream of continuing her education to advance a career, but she may not have adequate finances to quit her current job to attend college full-time. As her coach, you can encourage her to research all the available options, such as campuses that cater to full-time workers with online, evening, and/or weekend classes. Those options may seem obvious to us, but to the one who has lost hope of ever pursing her dreams, it could be an "aha!" moment.

However, some barriers are harder to recognize because they're not physical or external, but emotional and internal. These often prove to be the most challenging because they require the hard work of digging beneath the surface to expose them. Only then can the person name them and remove them. For example, someone may appear to be lazy and have little intrinsic motivation. We may think a stimulating speech to "just do it" should be all he needs to get started, but inside, he is wrestling with self-doubt because his parents constantly communicated that he was stupid, good for nothing, ugly, and would never amount to anything.

Many of our friends and clients long to make a difference and do something great, but they've internalized fears and doubts that have become seemingly impenetrable barriers. These types of emotional, deeply embedded barriers may seem like unmovable mountains, but with a lot of diligent work, they can definitely be removed!

Coaches need insight, skill, courage, and compassion to help others uncover barriers that have hindered their progress. And people need determination to overcome the emotional boulders that keep them weighed down, making them feel hopeless about ever fulfilling their dreams. Patiently and persistently, we help people overcome the barriers of a lack of confidence, insecurity, fear of rejection, past failures, abuse, self-doubt, and internalized negative messages. They can't do it alone. We have the privilege of stepping into their lives at a critical moment to build relationships, instill confidence, and help them replace the negative feelings and perceptions that hold them hostage.

The process of internal transformation is often slow and burdensome. As a coach, be patient. Remember that the negative thoughts, habits, and attitudes have been buried deep inside their lives for years. They are not removed easily, but we enjoy the reward of assisting others in digging, pulling, and tugging, so they make genuine progress.

At various points in our lives, we all encounter difficult barriers. Although others share similar situations and experiences, no two people are exactly the same, so there is no simple, clear, guaranteed, "cut-and-dried" way to overcome the obstacles we face. There are, however, steps we can take to overcome those obstacles and make them become stepping-stones to our success. We need courage and tenacity to take these steps to reach our destination.

First of all, we have to recognize the barrier standing in our way. It's not good enough to say, "I've always had this dream, but something is keeping me from it." You'll never see your dream become reality unless you can identify the barrier blocking you. Many people never reach their potential simply because they won't deal with the obstacle holding them back, which may be lack of commitment, education, motivation, emotional strength, willpower, self-control, etc.

Once you recognize the barrier(s), come up with a strategy of how to remove it. It didn't get in your way overnight, and it won't be removed instantly. It's a process. If your parents constantly told you that you wouldn't amount to anything, you won't just wake up one day with a desire to face the huge challenge of self-doubt. You have to surround yourself in a new environment of positive, honest people and their messages of hope. And when no one is there to pick you up, you need to develop new, positive beliefs that will keep you on the right track. Seeing life in a new way is like learning a new language—it's difficult and it takes discipline, but it's very rewarding.

Another step is to realize that failures *always* happen on the road to success. We need to remember that the average person experiences seven failures before celebrating a success! So failure isn't defeat; it's simply a realization of what doesn't work, which is an important step in achieving our goals. Great baseball players strike out much more than they hit home runs, but the home runs are what they're known for—not the failed attempts. To become positive, hopeful people, we need to change the negative way we look at failure. It has been said that it's better to fail at something than to succeed at nothing! We were all taught in school, "If at first you don't succeed, try, try again." This principle is effective and true for us at any age. With a fresh perspective and tenacious hope, we won't beat ourselves up so badly when we don't succeed in our first attempt.

After you identify the barrier and realize that failure is a part of the process on the road to success, the next step is to surround yourself with people who have reached similar goals. If you are financially in debt, you wouldn't want to hang out with others in the same shape. Instead, you would benefit from "rubbing shoulders" with others who have come from poverty into prosperity. From them, you will gain wisdom to achieve similar results. Stories are powerful motivators. A big step in reaching our goals is hearing about the journey others took to get where we want to be. Kick the naysayers out of your life and surround yourself with positive people who will support you on your journey!

Another step to overcoming barriers is to read inspiring books, listen to motivational podcasts, and surround yourself with positive energy. We all like to have "downtime" that doesn't require a lot of energy or thinking, but we are propelled toward success by the books we read, the messages we hear, and the attitudes of the people around us. Becoming a "couch potato" at the end of the workday will never get you out of a dead-end job. Get up, and do something to move to a new level. Remember that you only get one chance to go around in this life. Only you can decide if you are going to make yours count and accomplish what you were destined to do on this earth!

Many barriers keep people from accomplishing personal and professional goals. These barriers will do one of three things in our lives: stop us, distract us, or become stepping-stones to our goals. When we encounter barriers, we must be more determined than ever to succeed. If we believe in ourselves and develop an effective plan, facing obstacles enables us to get stronger, more creative, and more focused, so we can reach new heights. We have to trust what we do and then do it. Trust without action is useless. Determination drives us to put our hopes into action.

All goals and all decisions involve some element of risk. They may challenge our fears and doubts, or even change the original goal, but they should *never* discourage or stop us.

When setbacks occur . . .

- Re-evaluate your plan and make any necessary changes.
- Don't allow discouragement to set in.
- Remain flexible and confident when things don't go as planned.

- Stay motivated. Focus on the desired outcome, and continue to move toward the goal.
- Remember each stone you step on puts you a step closer to your dream.

All coaches and those they care about experience some form of barrier. When we find the courage to deal with our own, we'll be more equipped to help others with theirs. We can't give what we don't possess, so make a commitment to acquire the courage and skills to deal with whatever is holding you back.

Vengeance is having a videotape planted in your soul that cannot be turned off. It plays the painful scene over and over again inside your mind . . . And each time it plays you feel the clap of pain again . . . Forgiving turns off the videotape of pained memory. Forgiving sets you free.

—LEWIS SMEDES

CHAPTER 19

FOCUS ON CORE VALUES

The *Oxford Dictionary* defines values as "The principles or standards of behavior; one's judgment of what is important in life." Values are the things we deem important and the deeply held beliefs within us that direct the decisions we make concerning how we live, work, and relate with others. It is obvious that we are not born with values, so how do we develop them?

Sociologist Morris Massey identified three major periods during which values are developed: the Imprint Period, the Modeling Period, and the Socialization Period.[43] Massey described the Imprint Period, birth to age seven, as the sense of right and wrong that we adopt from our parents. He described the Modeling Period, ages eight to thirteen, where we copy others' values to see if they work for us. This could be anyone who makes an impression on our lives. Between the ages of

43 Morris Massey, "Values Development." Values Development, N.p., n.d. Web, 28 Sept. 2012, http://changingminds.org/explanations/values/values_development.htm.

thirteen and twenty-one, the Socialization Period, we are influenced by friends, peers, and the media. Clearly, values are developed from the experiences in our lives.

Once we identify our values, we tend to judge how successful and content we are by whether or not our lives line up with our value system. If we feel our personal or work habits align within our value boundaries, if you will, then there is little inward conflict. However, if we operate outside the value system we've established, then this is often a source of inward conflict.

Understanding our value system can help us establish priorities in our lives, both at work and at home. Although our values may change somewhat as we mature or have a family, they are fundamentally stable. For example, if as a youth you began to develop education as a value, then you are most likely going to pursue learning throughout your life and instill it in your children's lives, too. You'll even take on significant debt as a sacrifice along the way.

In defining your values, it may be helpful to reflect upon the times you were the most content. Sample questions you may ask are:

- "What were you doing at the time you were most content?"
- "What relationships were important then, and what external factors contributed to your contentment?"
- "Are there relationships you currently have that align within your value system?"
- "Are there relationships that do not align within your value system?"
- "Does your work life align? If not, how can you move toward your value system rather than away from it?"

- "If you never had to work another day, what would you want to do?"
- "If you have to create a community around you, whom would you include?"

As you answer questions such as these, it may become easier to determine your personal core values. Once you determine what your values are, think of ways you can reaffirm them in your present life.

Core values are not easily identified, and it can be challenging to come to terms with how your life and your value system align. You may find that some of the beliefs you live by are not your own beliefs. In fact, it may be that your actions are such because you are following someone else's expectations. Moreover, you may be frustrated in important relationships because you are projecting your values upon them. One thing is for sure, many life decisions are made based on what we value and what we do not.

PERSONAL CORE VALUES ARE:	PERSONAL CORE VALUES ARE NOT:
Our inward belief system by which we make life decisions.	Workplace norms and codes of conduct.
Things that are reflected in a person's life, such as attitude or character.	Society's norms.
How we nurture family and friendships.	Cultural norms.
How we relate with God.	Church or religious traditions.
How we make financial decisions.	Success as judged by others.

Everyone lives by core values—consciously or unconsciously. In order to live more intentionally, it helps to bring the values we already live by into our consciousness.

Below are two examples of the personal core values that Sam and Brenda Chand live by.

Family Core Values
- Be loyal to family members
- Believe in, uplift, and encourage family members
- Pray regularly for family members and intensify prayer when a member is struggling
- Love unconditionally even when you don't feel loved in return
- Don't speak negatively of family members to others
- Praise publicly, correct privately
- Be straightforward in all matters
- Trust

Financial Core Values
- Tithe on all income
- Pay bills in a timely manner
- No debt except mortgage
- Save and invest a predetermined amount
- Give generously
- Determine how much is enough to live on
- Make purchases based upon fulfillment of each of the criterion above
- Give the rest away

Note, these are very simple phrases. It is likely that you live based upon your own set of core values for several areas of life. Begin to jot down some areas of your life and core values about each of them. It will probably help to do this over several days and not just in one sitting. Knowing your core values will help you to become more intentional in decision-making and goal setting.

In *Christian Coaching: Helping Others Turn Potential into Reality*, Gary Collins offers a list of words and phrases that you can use to assist you in determining what you value most.[44] Please check the words/phrases that you value most and then add others as you think of them.

✓	WORD/PHRASE	✓	WORD/PHRASE	✓	WORD/PHRASE
	Accomplishment		Ambition		Authenticity
	Beauty		Being a model		Being in control
	Career		Caution		Collaboration
	Communication		Community		Compassion
	Competence		Competition		Consistency with biblical teaching
	Creativity		Determination		Diligence
	Efficacy		Encouragement		Enlightenment
	Excellence		Excitement		Experiencing pleasure
	Faithfulness		Family		Forgiveness
	Forward looking		Freedom		Frugality
	Fulfillment		Fun		Gentleness
	Genuineness		Good taste		Growth
	Hard work		Honesty		Humility
	Humor		Impacting people		Independence
	Influence		Inspiring others		Integrity

44 Gary R. Collins, Christian Coaching: Helping Others Turn Potential into Reality, (Colorado Springs, CO: NavPress, 2009), 367-368.

Joy		Lack of pretense		Love
Love of learning		Loyalty		Making money
Marriage		Mentoring		Nurturing
Obedience		Orderliness		Patience
Peace		Perfection		Performance
Persistence		Personal power		Physical vitality
Productivity		Purity		Quality
Recognition		Relaxation		Respect for life
Respect for people		Respect for the environment		Risk taking
Security		Self-esteem		Self-expression
Sensitivity		Servanthood		Service
Sexual fulfillment		Silence		Sincerity
Solitude		Spiritual growth		Stability
Success		Temperance		Tolerance
Tongue control		Tranquility		Trust
Winning		Worship		

For further exploration of values, principles, and qualities, feel free to glean from the following website: healthskills.files.wordpress.com/2010/08values-worksheet-river.doc.

CHAPTER 20

THE ELUSIVE "BALANCED LIFE"

CASE STUDY

Like many working moms, Lynn was incredibly diligent at work and poured out everything she had left at the end of the day for her two children, ages twelve and eight. She tried cutting down on sleep, so she had more time to prepare for the next day's tasks, but that left her feeling exhausted and irritable. She read books on efficiencies, but they only made her more obsessive-compulsive. She asked her husband to do more around the house, but he said that wasn't the solution to her problem. She resented his unwillingness to help, but in her heart she knew he was right.

Weekly . . . and sometimes daily . . . Lynn made solemn commitments to go home at 5:00 every day, take her thirty minutes for lunch, and not open her laptop at night or on weekends, but these vows were soon broken.

In spite of her dedication to every person and every responsibility, she felt like a total failure. She told her best friend, "I can't get everything done at work, I'm not a good mom because I'm too distracted, and my marriage . . . My husband says he doesn't even know me anymore!"

For some people, a balanced life seems like a dream beyond their grasp. They've tried to achieve a semblance of balance, but it hasn't worked out. Actually, it's possible for all of us, but we need some handles on the problem. To achieve balance in everyday life, we need to acquire skills to manage our time, families, careers, health, and recreation. In this chapter, several key elements will be identified and described, and we'll discover ways to integrate them to create and maintain a healthy sense of balance.

TIME MANAGEMENT

A few years ago, the creators of new technologies promised their inventions would make our lives richer and more relaxed. Certainly, productivity has increased, but people are more stressed than ever by the demands of everyday responsibilities. The technologies have only made it easier to communicate the demands! The days are over of going to work, coming home in the evening, preparing supper, everyone gathering around the table for dinner, watching a little television together, and then calling it a night. We don't live in Ozzie and Harriet's house anymore! Today, most families are running ragged with activities long after the school day and work are over. Relaxed conversations seem to have gone extinct with the dinosaurs. Most families run from one event to the next, grabbing something to eat and talking only about cramming in the next event. They rush to sports activities, piano lessons, dance recitals, tutoring programs, parties, and all kinds of other "necessary" events. A couple of minutes in the line at a fast-food drive-thru takes the place of supper with the family at home. Parents feel stressed out and wish they could clone themselves to get everything done on their "to-do" lists. They hit the ground running way before daybreak, only to fall into bed way beyond sunset, feeling disappointed that they didn't accomplish all they set out to do for the day.

Sooner or later, we realize that if we don't take control of our lives, our lives will easily take control of (and destroy) us! Is it possible to get off this maddening treadmill? Yes, but it's not easy. Living a healthy, meaningful, balanced life requires planning, setting priorities, and the courage to make hard choices. Here are some crucial guidelines:

1) Have a Plan

In every field of business, we would consider it foolish for someone to launch a venture or manage an existing process without having a sound plan. Our lives aren't less important or less complicated than many businesses, yet many people believe they can make decisions "on the fly." In all aspects of life—careers, family, physical health, and recreation—we need sound, workable plans. And we need a global plan that puts all these elements together, so we can enjoy balance and fulfillment.

The Bible tells us that no one builds a house without counting the cost in advance. You may not be in the process of building a new home, but each day, you're building your destiny. Without a plan, you set yourself up for failure. It's like going to the grocery store without taking the time to make a list of the items you need. Quite often, we roam around the aisles wondering if we need this or that, and after wasting far too much time, we arrive at home realizing we forgot the main ingredient for a recipe. Our bag, though, is full. We purchased things we didn't need and had no intention of buying when we left home. Managing our time is similar to managing any other part of life. We begin by setting priorities and crafting a plan to accomplish those priorities. To do that, we realize we have to say "yes" to some things and "no" to others. And some of the things on the list are more important than others. We can't do it all, and not all of the important things are supremely important.

2) Designate and Delegate

Some of the important things that need to get done don't necessarily have to be done by us. We shouldn't be afraid to ask for help. When we rely only on our talents and time, we soon get stressed out. In most cases, help is available if we'll only ask. Some of us are simply too proud to ask for help. We want to look strong, in control, and supremely competent. But this kind of pride alienates people and creates more stress for us. It's foolish and destructive. "No man (or woman) is an island," so stop trying to do everything yourself; allow others to take part of the load off your shoulders.

3) Learn to Say "No"

When we feel stressed, everything seems urgent and necessary—until we crash, and then nothing seems important any more. Establishing priorities necessarily means some things are more important than others. We can't do it all, and we can't do very many things with excellence. Perfectionists drive themselves and everyone around them crazy. And those who are under a pile of undifferentiated pressures can't distinguish one priority from another. From time to time, we need to step back and reassess our life's trajectory, reaffirm our values, and find the courage to establish our priorities again. We don't have to volunteer for every job. We don't have to do everything with the utmost excellence. We don't have to add another responsibility to prove ourselves to those who are watching. We can say "No," and in fact, we *must* say "no" to some things if we're going to survive and thrive.

When we set priorities and stick to them, we may disappoint some people. It's almost inevitable. But we choose to invest our time and energies in the people, goals, and tasks that we value most. In this, we have satisfaction and fulfillment. However, there are ways to turn people *down* without turning them *off*. Remember when you were a child? The threat was always hovering over your head that a friend would say, "If you don't do what I want to do, then I won't be your friend!" As adults, we need to realize that our real friends will *still* be our friends whether we can attend every gathering, run every errand, or do every favor asked of us. Learning to say "no" is essential if we are to reduce stress, value people, and find balance in our lives.

4)   Give Your Meetings a Time Limit

Parkinson's law is that a job expands to fill the time allotted to it. This is certainly true for meetings. If we have an open-ended time frame, people talk incessantly, add extraneous details, and wander off course. Quite often, these meetings become social events with endless chatting, gossip, and banter, throwing the day completely off course. When you schedule a meeting—virtually any meeting—set a time limit. Create the reputation of beginning *and* ending on time. If you're asked to attend a meeting set by someone else, politely inform the leader in advance that you would like it to conclude at a certain time because you have other commitments. This strategy isn't always possible (especially if the top brass is calling the meeting), but don't be shy about asking for an ending time to a meeting. If you can get the leader to agree to a time limit, you can be fully devoted to the goals of the meeting, and you'll have time to fulfill your other responsibilities. Setting limits on meetings can greatly reduce stress.

5) Schedule Some Time for Rest or Leisure

Many studies show how rest and relaxation positively affect our happiness and success. Some people are workaholics. Those who are watching may think it's noble that the hardworking person is so devoted to work responsibilities, but beyond a certain point, it's pathological. Studies also show that the accumulation of wealth and power isn't ultimately satisfying. Relationships, leisure, and serving others are the factors that provide the highest level of satisfaction and meaning. Relentless acquisition is a never-ending rat race. Gaining more money, possessions, and power satisfies only for a moment. Then the person realizes someone else has still more, so the rat race speeds up, so the person can catch up. Besides, many wealthy, powerful people spend much of their time and money taking care of all their possessions instead of enjoying them. Our children won't remember the money we spent on designer clothes, fancy cars, and lavish vacations we provided for them. But they'll vividly remember the *time* we invest in them in spite of our busy days. Time is a gift. We are to cherish it, use it wisely, and remember that the amount we waste will never be given back to us. Schedule some time in each day, regardless how busy it is, to not only count your blessings, but surround yourself with those blessings!

FAMILY PRIORITIES

If a person succeeds in a career but his family is full of bitterness or distance, he doesn't feel successful at all. Conversely, if a person's family life is rich, warm, and meaningful, she can endure disappointments in other parts of her life with poise and confidence. Strong family relationships are a solid foundation on which to build the rest of life. Without them, everything—even prestige, wealth, comfort, and power—seems meaningless. A balanced family life can be described as the ability to successfully combine your family, your career, and yourself into your twenty-four-hour day and still live to tell about it. For men and women, today's demands of work and family life can be overwhelming.

There is no single formula for attaining a balanced family. We have different personalities, different situations, and different stages of family life. For instance, the demands of raising kids in junior high are different from caring for infants, launching college graduates into an adult world, or caring for elderly parents. And the issues surrounding blended families can be incredibly complex. People have to assess their relationships and current circumstances, and then chart a wise course to make their families a priority, balancing family with other important goals. The key is developing creative solutions to our families' opportunities and challenges. Ironically, the same strategies we use at work—such as planning, organizing, communicating, delegating, and yes, even saying "no" to some things—can be used effectively at home.

To creatively and thoughtfully find balance in our family life, we need to recognize the devastating impact of perfectionism. Families are complicated, living organisms, not engine parts or quantifiable elements of a business plan. Relationships are fluid and messy, but they provide more joy and meaning than any other area of life. To find balance, talk to the people in your family. Invite their input, and ask them to find creative solutions to life's demands. Look for ways to make compromises without shortchanging anyone. You want every person to feel valued and respected.

We all have only twenty-four hours for each day, so we have to set priorities. The choices we make will determine the level of each day. There is no perfect job, no perfect performance, and no perfect family. We need to be realistic, creative, and determined to find balance. Let's look at some ways to approach our goal of a balanced family life:

1)   Establish Priorities

Before we can begin to work toward a balanced family life, we have to establish our priorities. Some of these can be our spouse, children, work, church, relationships with friends, hobbies, passions, etc.

2)   Establish Core Values and Live by Them

Our core values determine our goals, our priorities, and ultimately, the worth of our lives. Quite often, our level of satisfaction at the end of each day is determined by how well we lived by (or compromised) our core values. Stress and anxiety can often be the result of feeling disappointed or guilty about decisions we've made that violated our core value system.

3)   Establish Limits and Boundaries

Limits determine how far we are willing to go in taking responsibility for others' feelings, attitudes, and behavior. Boundaries are an imaginary line of protection we draw to protect us from the negative influence other people can have on us. Each person must determine acceptable and unacceptable behavior—ours toward others and theirs toward us. Boundaries and limits also define how we take charge of our time and resources and how we get in touch with our feelings. When we have clear, established boundaries, we can say "no" without confusion or guilt. We need to remind ourselves often that limits and boundaries are necessary for balancing work and family.

4) Create Time for Yourself

Being a good spouse, parent, friend, and professional means being good to yourself first. Self-validation and self-care are important. Find ways to relax and reduce the effects of stress. Taking some time off for yourself will not only benefit you, but it will benefit everyone and everything in your life. Some important ways to create time for yourself include:

- Get organized at home and at work. Create short-term and long-term priority lists, maintain a personal and family calendar, and delegate responsibilities when you can.
- Be flexible. Don't allow stress and guilt to overtake you when things don't get done. Understand that unplanned incidents often occur—especially with children.
- Realize that you can't save the world. Taking on other people's goals and responsibilities will only sabotage your own family's balance.

5) Recognize the Signs of Imbalance

Emotional highs and lows are often indicators of an unbalanced family life. Other indicators are fatigue, depression, resentment, unhappy family members, and chronic dissatisfaction with work or family.

6) Carve Out and Treasure Quality Family Time

Spend quality, focused time with your family. When you're with them, give them your full attention. Develop meaningful rituals you can all look forward to. Create relationships with your spouse and children that are not incidental, but rather, instrumental to your sense of joy and fulfilment.

CAREER

In his article, "Diagnosing Hurry Sickness" in *Leadership* magazine, John Ortberg identified two common signs of stress: speeding up and multitasking:

1) "Speeding up. You are haunted by the fear that you don't have enough time to do what needs to be done. You try to read faster, lead board meetings more efficiently, write [business plans or emails] on the fly. . . ."

2) "Multiple-tasking. You find yourself doing or thinking more than one thing at a time. The car is a favorite place for this. Hurry-sick [leaders] may drive, eat, drink coffee, listen to tapes for [sic] ideas, shave or apply make-up, direct [sic] business on the car phone—all at the same time. Or they may try to watch TV, read *Leadership*, eat dinner, and carry on a phone conversation simultaneously."[45]

---

45 John Ortberg, "Diagnosing Hurry Sickness," Leadership, Fall, 1998.

It can be tempting to rack up hours at work, especially if you're trying to earn a promotion or manage an ever-increasing workload—or simply keep your head above water. All work is hard some of the time, and some work is hard all of the time. If we're depleting our resources in our careers, we won't have anything to give to our families, and we won't take care of our bodies.

Consider the consequences of poor work-life balance:

- **Fatigue.** When you're chronically tired, your abilities to work productively and think clearly inevitably suffer—which could take a toll on your professional reputation and keep you from being enthusiastic about your family.

- **Lost time with friends and loved ones.** If you're working too much, you might miss important family events or milestones. This can leave you feeling left out and will probably harm your most valued relationships. It's also difficult to build friendships if you're always working.

- **Unrealistic expectations.** If you regularly work extra hours, you might be given more responsibility—which could lead to additional concerns and challenges. Bosses love perfectionists and workaholics, but they eventually burn out.

THE BASICS

Most coaches haven't been trained in the health sciences, so we should avoid making clinical diagnoses. If those who have come to us for help are showing signs of stress, anxiety, loss of sleep or sleeping too much, hypertension, significant weight gain or loss, and other symptoms, we should refer them to a doctor. Most of our friends or clients, however, simply need reminders to use common sense.

- **Diet:** We can ask people to chart what they eat for a week, and then analyze the quantity and quality of their diets. In many cases, people are shocked to realize the poor choices they've made—choices they may have been making for years. Find a health-related site that provides clear, simple instructions for eating a healthy diet—but avoid arguments about the effectiveness of different diets.

- **Exercise.** Some people work out five or more days a week in a gym, but good exercise doesn't have to cost much money. Some good walking shoes are all most people need—along with the determination to walk at least thirty minutes a day three or four times a week. And these walks shouldn't be casual strolls. People need to walk fast enough to get their heart rates up a bit. Again, most of us aren't experts in this area. If the person is significantly overweight or has other health problems, refer to a physician for directions about exercise.

- **Sleep.** The pressures of life, instant connections with people, and cable news have eroded the amount of sleep many people get today. It can begin with staying up a little later and getting up a little earlier, but many people can't go to sleep or stay asleep. Today, sleep deprivation is an epidemic in our culture. A WebMD article by Jeannie Lerche Davis reports, "Yet there's strong evidence that lost sleep is a serious matter. The Sleep in America polls and several large studies have linked sleep deficits with poor work performance, driving accidents, relationship problems, and mood problems like anger and depression. A growing list of health risks has been documented in recent studies, too. Heart disease, diabetes, and obesity have all been linked with chronic sleep loss."[46]

When we talk to people about these issues, we may be saving their marriages, restoring relationships with children, advancing their careers, and even saving their lives. We won't be able to speak with clarity and validity, however, if we aren't practicing what we preach.

46 Jeanie Lerche Davis, "The Toll of Sleep Loss in America," WebMD, www.webmd.com/sleep-disorders/guide/toll-of-sleep-loss-in-america (16 December 2012).

CHAPTER 21

ESTABLISHING YOUR MISSION, VISION, AND PURPOSE

Some coaches have observed that many people live with a secret deadly fear. They dread coming to the end having lived a meaningless life. Finding a mission, and then fulfilling it, is perhaps the most important activity in a person's life. For any enterprise, including your role as a professional coach, it's important to establish a crystal-clear mission, vision, and purpose. In professional literature, some begin with vision and fill it out with elements of the mission, but others view mission as the starting point. The three are often considered synonyms, but they're distinctly different, and they build on one another.

> The very essence of leadership is that you have to
> have vision. You can't blow an uncertain trumpet.

**—THEODORE HESBURGH, FORMER PRESIDENT OF
NOTRE DAME UNIVERSITY FOR 35 YEARS**

MISSION

A *mission* is a picture of the future, where the organization (or your career) is going. When the goals are accomplished, this is what success looks like. By its nature, it's inspirational. In fact, if it doesn't inspire people to dream bigger and be more enthused, it's not big enough or clear enough. To capture people's attention, it needs to be no longer than what's written on a business card—and can be read without a magnifying glass!

A mission statement is a clear statement of the reason for existence—for a person, a family, or a company. It charts the overarching direction. In coaching, we help each person define his or her mission in life, and we may also assist people in crafting an organizational mission. For individuals and organizations, having a clearly articulated mission statement provides a template for decisions and a yardstick to evaluate every activity.[47]

People who aren't sure where they're going suffer from a variety of problems. Some become stuck and can't make decisions. Others make snap decisions and often change their minds. Still others drift from one new direction to another because every new idea seems equally

---

47 Laurie Beth Jones, The Path: Creating Your Mission Statement for Work and for Life, (New York, NY: Hyperion, 1996), 11.

valid. All of these people share a couple of things in common: they're confused and frustrated.

But life doesn't have to be this way. Clarifying your mission can help you chart a clear course for the future and navigate relationships. All of us have a tendency to drift, to forget, and to go off course. Writing a compelling mission statement reminds us of our commitments and values. It's essential if we're to live a full, meaningful life.

To craft a powerful mission statement, it should have these three characteristics:

1) It's a single sentence.

2) It's clear.

3) It's easy to memorize.

Most of the outstanding leaders in history have had mission statements that fit these three criteria. Abraham Lincoln's mission was to preserve the Union. Franklin Roosevelt's was to end the Depression and win World War II. Nelson Mandela's mission was to end racial apartheid in South Africa. Mother Teresa's was to show mercy and compassion to the dying in India. And Joan of Arc's mission was to free France from oppression.

In creating mission statements, we find a paradox: The greater the mission, the more easily it can be stated. If our mission is miniscule, it won't capture our hearts. Fuzzy mission statements are easily forgotten or ignored, but clear ones remind us every day: This is why I'm alive! This is why my life counts!

A compelling mission statement is a firm foundation for every aspect of life. With it, we have direction and motivation; without it, we wander.

A person's sense of personal mission is the natural extension of vision, values, and roles. Let's put it this way: It's inconceivable that a person's compelling mission would be in conflict with his vision for the future, his core values, and his roles in his family, business, and community. These things must align for the mission to make sense. Vision, values, and roles provide the context for the expressions of emotions, expectations and experiences, and these lead to a life of happiness, satisfaction and significance.[48]

How do you know if your mission in life
is finished? If you're still alive, it isn't.

—RICHARD BACH

People need a reason to live, a benchmark for progress, and a template for their choices. When a mission statement captures a person's heart, it opens a wide door to the future. Then, every role and relationship take on added meaning, and every choice becomes clearer.

Haas and Madson observe, "Your mission, integrated with your vision and your values, dictates what's important in your life. You are naturally the most productive when you are working from your heart, investing the only life you have in what you care about the most."[49]

VISION

A *vision* defines the actionable components of the person's goals or the organization's work. It answers the questions of who, what, when, why,

---

48 Jones, 3, 5-6, ix.
49 Hass and Madson, 183.

and how. It clarifies the target audience, the market, and the concrete steps that will be taken to pursue the mission. The vision makes immediate goals clear, with responsibilities and timelines.

Mission is the map; *vision* is the road to get to the destination. Your vision includes the nitty-gritty details that help you make real progress. Discovering and implementing your personal vision requires the process of self-discovery, establishing specific goals, and continually fine-tuning your direction. It's a dynamic and sometimes complex process. Your vision is increasingly refined as your purpose becomes clearer, and your purpose becomes clearer as you experience successes and failures, triumphs and defeats, joys and sorrows. A person's vision is a dynamic, growing thing.

Very few people have a clear vision from the outset of their lives and careers. All of the great leaders mentioned responded to specific challenges they faced. Situations in our lives change, too, so we need to come back again and again to assess our personal vision statement. At least once a year, we should take time to reevaluate our life's direction and course. The essence of vision is the ability to see into the future, to envision a desired destiny. Vision is seeing the future before it becomes reality.[50] Vision is how you see yourself fulfilling your mission.

My mission is:
When I become aware, I must share.
My vision is:
When I become aware, I must share through teaching, coaching, mentoring, and modeling.
—BRENDA C. CHAND

---

50 Myles Munroe, The Principles and Power of Vision, (New Kensington, PA: Whitaker House, 2003), 17.

Merriam-Webster's definition of vision includes: "a thought, concept, or object formed by the imagination, the act or power of imagination, and unusual discernment or foresight."[51]

To craft a vision statement, follow these steps:[52]

1) Step One: Eliminate Distractions

Get away from distractions and responsibilities, and allow yourself some uninterrupted time to reflect. Charting a future shouldn't be rushed!

2) Step Two: Find Your True Self

Very few people are self-aware. The vast majority of us wear masks to cover our insecurities, and we are sometimes clueless about our hidden motives, desires, and dreams. The more we know the truth about ourselves—the good, the bad, and the ugly—the more we can accentuate our skills and overcome our flaws. Reality can be threatening, but facing it is a sure source of progress. To peel away a few layers of self-deception, think about these questions:

- What gives you the most joy, pleasure, and fulfillment?
- What causes you to experience anxiety?
- What do you hope no one finds out about you?
- Who are the people you're honest with (or at least, more honest with)?

---

51 Merriam-Webster Online, "Vision," http://www.merriam-webster.com/dictionary/vision (14 October 2012).
52 Adapted from "How to Write Your Personal Vision Plan," www.slideshare.net.

3) Step Three: Find Your True Vision

A person's compelling vision transcends the grind of daily life. To find our true vision, we have to push ourselves to dream big dreams. Take time to answer these penetrating questions:

- How do you want your life to count?
- What inspires you so much you can't stop dreaming about it?
- What do you want to do more than anything else, even if you're not paid for it?
- What kind of impact do you want to leave on your family, your organization, and your community?
- In what way would you like the world to be different because you were here?

4) Step Four: Discover Your True Motivation

A vision is never self-focused. The paradox of meaning in life is that we gain the most when we give, we live by dying to our selfish desires, and we gain real power when we humbly serve. We were meant to make a difference, not to dominate. We are most fulfilled when we pour our lives into serving, caring, and loving others. To discover your true motivations, reflect on these questions:

- How does your vision help others? Be specific.
- How will their lives be happier and more fulfilled if you follow your dreams?
- Be honest: How much of your motivation is to achieve power, prestige, and possessions?
- Who do you know who truly lives and leads to serve others? What's attractive about that person? What's confusing?

- What changes need to happen in your heart, so your motivations are less self-absorbed and you're more of a servant?

5) **Step Five: Identify Your Principles**

Your principles comprise your philosophy of life. They are the benchmarks for integrity, honesty, strength, and kindness. Principles guide your choices in every aspect of life: family, finances, career, friendships, and every other sphere of life. The next section explores the connection between principles and vision.

A VISION'S PRINCIPLES AND PROCESS

Sight is a function of the eyes, but vision is a function of the heart. J. Oswald Sanders observed, "Eyes that look are common, but eyes that see are rare." This means that we may look at our relationships and careers but fail to see beneath the surface. Sight is the ability to see things *as they are*; vision is the capacity to see things *as they could be*.[53]

Trying to construct a life without a clear vision is like a contractor trying to build a house without a blueprint. He may have all the resources at the site, but he doesn't know how to put them together. It's a sure recipe for frustration! We need a specific plan to fulfill our vision. The plan includes principles and process.

A number of authors provide lists of principles and processes in understanding and clarifying a person's vision. Consider these:

- Vision is confidence in a future reality.
- Vision is progressive.
- Vision is a function of mission and leads to a powerful purpose.
- Vision is always challenging, threatening, and uncomfortable.

---

53 Munroe, The Principles and Power of Vision, 11.

- Vision inspires.
- Vision is never satisfied with the status quo.
- Vision always builds people up, never tears them down.
- Vision drives planning.
- Vision captures hearts.
- Vision is fulfilled in stages.
- Vision is essential for leaders.
- Vision propels action.

A powerful vision exists in tandem with the daily mission and a clear sense of purpose, which together produce intrinsic motivation. It doesn't instantaneously appear. It always involves a process. The sequencing of the process may or may not be exactly this ten-step model, but it will involve this general flow:

1) Vision often begins by recognizing a need.
2) Vision is the product of a compassionate heart and a big dream to meet the need.
3) Vision becomes clearer over time.
4) Vision is shared and adopted by others.
5) Vision doesn't diminish as it takes shape.
6) Vision is detailed, targeted, reasonable, and sequential.
7) Vision produces a comprehensive plan.
8) Vision is continually evaluated and revised.
9) Vision generates momentum with every step of progress.
10) Vision produces celebrations.

A vision of the future isn't tangible—not yet anyway—but a powerful, clear vision seems just as real as today's physical world. When a vision captures our hearts, we live for its fulfillment. Vivid dreams of the future feel like present reality.

PURPOSE

A *purpose* is the driving determination to make a difference. In an article in *Forbes*, Jen Croneberger comments:

> *In my experience, an organization's purpose is best found by asking, as a company, why you are doing the work you are doing. What great problem are you solving, or what movement are you championing? If you don't do it, what are the consequences? Who loses? Or who will do it instead? Why do you all show up for this company and not the one across the street? . . . When a solid human brand leads people to a conversation that says, without hesitation, "I love my job. I love what I do. I love my company, and I love the people I work for/with," purpose is usually at the center.*

And she summarizes the three:

> *Vision is the picture. Mission is the road map to get there. Purpose is the feeling that everyone, from the CEO to the janitor, has when you accomplish what you set out to do. Purpose is when the values are driven by certain behaviors that create the kind of culture that is human-centric. And those behaviors create the feeling we want, not only when we have accomplished the big goals and achieved the outcomes we wanted, but in the process of doing so.[54]*

---

54 "Vision, Mission, and Purpose: The Difference," Jen Croneberger, Forbes, March 4, 2020, https://www.forbes.com/sites/forbescoachescouncil/2020/03/04/vision-mission-and-purpose-the-difference/?sh=7063bee3280e

The purpose of our lives is more compelling than personal fulfillment, peace of mind, or happiness. It defines our legacy: the way we shape people's lives today and the impact we leave behind when we're gone. It gives clearer, sharper definition to our reason for getting up each morning. Mission and vision let us know our lives matter; our purpose describes specifically *how* they matter.

Merriam-Webster defines purpose as "something set up as an object or end to be obtained; intention." Dictionary.com defines it as "the reason for which something exists or is done, made, used." Unfortunately, many people live with nagging self-doubt and muffled fear that their lives don't really matter at all. They wander aimlessly.

A sense of purpose isn't an aftermarket add-on—it's essential if we're to have full and meaningful lives. We crave purpose like we crave delicious food. We can't live without a sense of relevance and significance. The search for purpose is our ultimate pursuit. Whether we realize it or not, this drive motivates us to enter relationships, take risks, and give our lives to a great cause. Before we discover our purpose, our lives have no meaning, because purpose is the source of true fulfillment.[55]

The search for the purpose of life confuses many people because they start at the wrong point. Many think of personal rewards, comforts, and accolades as their purpose in life, but these ultimately leave people feeling empty and flat. Our life's purpose is based on a vision for making a difference, but it goes one step further. Purpose defines the impact. It asks:

- Who are the people you love, lead, and serve?
- What role do you uniquely play in each of their lives?

---

55 Myles Munroe, In Pursuit of Purpose, (Shippensburg, PA: Destiny Image, 1992), foreword, preface.

- What impact can you have on each of them to make their lives as meaningful as possible?
- What is your specific plan to have this impact?
- If you don't invest time, love, and resources into their lives, what will they lose? What will you lose?[56]

Rick Warren, the author of *The Purpose Driven Life*, explains that people enjoy five great benefits of living a life of purpose:

1) Knowing your purpose *gives meaning*.
A sense of purpose gives us energy to take advantage of opportunities, strength to face adversities, and wisdom to handle every situation. When our lives have purpose, we know that we are making a difference—and it feels right.

2) Knowing your purpose *simplifies* life.
We experience an incredible array of competing interests in every part of our lives. When we don't have a clear sense of purpose, they all look equally valid—and equally confusing. We feel frantic or overwhelmed—and sometimes both! Clarifying our purpose gives us a framework of wisdom to be able to distinguish between things that make sense and things that don't. Life is complex even with a compelling purpose, and it's a zoo without it.

3) Knowing your purpose *focuses* your life.
Instead of drifting in confusion, a sense of purpose rivets our attention on the things we've designated as most important. We become more

---

56 Adapted from Rick Warren, The Purpose Driven Life, (Grand Rapids, MI: Zondervan 2002), 17.

effective by being more selective. Without a clear purpose, we change directions, jobs, and relationships, hoping each change will finally make us happy and fill the emptiness in our hearts.

4)   Knowing your purpose *motivates* you.
Purpose inevitably produces passion. We may not express our passion in the same ways, but all of us—introverts and extroverts, visionaries and managers—put fuel into our life's engine when our purpose is crystal clear.

5)   Knowing your purpose *prepares* you.
A clear purpose gives us the incentive to devote adequate resources to planning. When we know our lives matter, we can't afford to assume good things will magically happen. We invest in time, money, energy, and other resources to prepare ourselves to be our best. Our legacy is at stake. It's not that we live to be remembered, but we'll be remembered if we make a difference in people's lives.[57]

PRINCIPLES OF PURPOSE

Principles are foundational truths with universal applications. Four key concepts apply to our purpose:

1)   The uniqueness of purpose.
Every inventor or manufacturer begins with purpose. He establishes the purpose of the product or service before beginning production. In the same way, a person's purpose is his unique driving force of meaning.

---

57 Adapted from Warren, 30-33.

When you uncover and discover your unique contribution, you'll devote everything to fulfill your purpose.

2) Everything in life has purpose.

Life may seem random, and in fact, it may be random and meaningless for many people. Those who have a sense of purpose, though, look at every moment through its lens. Every moment, every goal, every interaction, and every activity is important because it contributes or detracts from the ultimate meaning in our lives.

3) Wherever purpose isn't clear, entropy is inevitable.

Entropy is the tendency toward randomness. When you throw a hundred pennies into the air, the pattern they form on the ground is fairly random. But if you intentionally place the pennies in a particular pattern, they can spell words, form a portrait, or create a design. In the same way, our lives don't have to look like pennies have been thrown into the air. We have the privilege and responsibility to define the direction and pattern of our futures.

4) Purpose is the key to fulfillment.

Purpose drives performance, which then produces satisfaction. When we have a sense of purpose, we can measure the value and impact of our lives. When we see our vision fulfilled, we are ecstatic; and when we fall short, we can make adjustments. A deep, wonderful sense of satisfaction never just happens. It's the product of living according to a definite purpose. Apart from purpose, life often seems fatalistic. In essence, you will never experience true fulfillment until you are executing the purpose you were born to accomplish.[58]

BENEFITS OF PURPOSE

We enjoy several specific benefits of defining our purpose in life and living to achieve it, including:

1) Purpose gives confidence.

It assures us that what we are on the right track. When we discover our purpose for our lives, we can be confident we will succeed.

2) Purpose provides protection.

A sense of purpose keeps us from drifting into self-destructive behaviors and meaningless pursuits.

3) Purpose empowers perseverance.

When we know we're going in the right direction for the right reasons, we have the strength to face obstacles and the patience to wait for our vision to become a reality.

4) Purpose produces and maintains objectivity.

It's easy to live in a dreamland of hopes and possibilities, but a clear sense of purpose causes us to be ruthlessly honest. We can't afford to be blind to the opportunities or the obstacles. Too much is at stake!

---

58 Adapted from Munroe, In Pursuit of Purpose, 8, 27-29, 31, 38.

5)   Purpose sustains contentment.

Inevitably, we experience ups and downs on the road to our destiny. If our purpose isn't clear, we become anxious and angry. When it remains clear, however, we have a strong foundation of courage and hope. No matter what, we can be content.[59]

Mission is the destination, vision is the map, and purpose is the engine in the car. You need all three to get where you want to go.

---

59 Adapted from Munroe, In Pursuit of Purpose, 95-96, 98-99, 102, 103.

CHAPTER 22

BECOMING A CHANGE AGENT

As coaches, we have the unique role of stepping into people's lives at a moment of need or opportunity. They have come to us because they want help navigating the turbulent waters of change, and we have the privilege of launching them into the future. To be an effective agent of change . . .

- Always preserve the reputation of the past. All change represents a critique of the past. That's why it's so important that you frequently praise past friends or clients and all the work they did. Their success is your heritage.

- Move slowly. Take time to know each person. Learn their history. It can be a valuable ally in moving them into change.

- Rally broad-based support for change. Don't expect everyone to support your friend or client's changes. Opposition may come from expected sources (such as people who have already been critical) or unexpected ones (a spouse or friend who prefers the status quo). As a coach, you can provide a strong dose of realism about the process and the cost of change, and you can be a rock of support through it all.

- Change is painful, so be ready to walk them through the pain. There will be many bad days during the change process.
- Challenge those you coach to come up with their best ideas. Treat every idea with respect and become their biggest cheerleader.
- Challenge and empower every person you coach. Never be satisfied with the minimum acceptable level of quality from them. "Just getting by" doesn't cut it—for them or for us.
- Occasionally look back at the progress they have made. They need to be aware of how far they've come as well as how far they still have to go. Give them an opportunity to look back and say, "Can you believe that? Look how far we've come together!"

Humility is the only true wisdom by
which we prepare our minds for all
the possible changes of life.
—GEORGE ARLISS

By the nature of how coaching begins, coaches are in a one-up position. People come to us because they need help, and they trust us to provide the help they need. Being in a position of authority gives us an identity as "the one people count on," and it provides an adrenaline rush that feels really good. But we lead by serving, we treat people with honor and respect, and we "think more highly of others than of ourselves." If we don't understand this perspective, we'll use our knowledge and skills to "fix" people, maintaining our one-up position.

Years ago, Robert Greenleaf coined the term "servant leader." This concept perfectly describes the role of coaches. We're asked to step in to lead people to the next step in their growth and development, but we're there to serve the person's interests and respect the person's pace, not to force our ideas and schedule. We have a unique privilege to be confidantes and cheerleaders, great listeners and dream-reinforcers. Greenleaf explained:

> *The servant-leader is servant first. . . . It begins with the natural feeling that one wants to serve, to serve first. Then conscious choice brings one to aspire to lead. That person is sharply different from one who is leader first, perhaps because of the need to assuage an unusual power drive or to acquire material possessions. . . .*
>
> *A servant-leader focuses primarily on the growth and well-being of people and the communities to which they belong. While traditional leadership generally involves the accumulation and exercise of power by one at the "top of the pyramid," servant leadership is different. The servant-leader shares power, puts the needs of others first, and helps people develop and perform as highly as possible.*[60]

In another article, Greenleaf said that this kind of heart is essential for people to thrive. It's not ancillary, and it's not optional. He wrote with conviction:

---

60 Robert K. Greenleaf, "The Servant as Leader," 1970, https://www.greenleaf.org/what-is-servant-leadership/.

> *This is my thesis: caring for persons, the more able and the less able serving each other, is the rock upon which a good society is built. Whereas, until recently, caring was largely person to person, now most of it is mediated through institutions—often large, complex, powerful, impersonal; not always competent; sometimes corrupt. If a better society is to be built, one that is more just and more loving, one that provides greater creative opportunity for its people, then the most open course is to raise both the capacity to serve and the very performance as servant of existing major institutions by new regenerative forces operating within them.[61]*

Each time we answer a call, each time we hear someone's story, and each time we ask powerful questions to clarify someone's direction, we need to remember that we're servants . . . first, last, and in between.

---

61 Ibid.

Common Topics in Coaching

CHAPTER 23

INSTILLING
SELF-CONFIDENCE

To some degree, those who lack self-confidence are consumed by fear—the "what-ifs" and "if onlys" that cloud their thinking and diminish their hopes. The expressions of this fear come in many different shapes and sizes. Some analyze things to death before making a decision—if they ever make it. Others fail to think about the consequences; they dive into new ventures and just hope they work out better than the last one. And some feel so insecure that they don't trust themselves to think, plan, and execute a strategy. They always look to others to make their decisions for them.

In every sphere of life, confidence is essential—not arrogance that demands attention and control, but something far deeper: the inner strength that comes from a bedrock of security in our talents, experiences, and relationships. When we enjoy this kind of security, opportunities to change aren't as threatening, challenges don't seem insurmountable, and failure doesn't have the last word.

How is it possible that two people face similar opportunities, and one responds with courage and confidence, while the other procrastinates and misses the chance of a lifetime? And how is it possible that two people experience crushing difficulties, and one finds a way to learn life's most important lessons, while the other wallows in self-pity and resentment? At every point in life, we have multiple options. Those who learn to master themselves become the masters of their circumstances.

In the 1960s Bandura and Walters developed the social learning approach that has a basic assumption: "People are capable of self-directed behavior change." Self-efficacy (which is another term for self-confidence) is a component of the social learning approach. The concept of self-efficacy has been explored since the late 1970s and brought to the forefront largely through Bandura's research. Self-efficacy can be defined as "the individual's belief or expectation that he or she can master a situation and bring about desired change."[62] An individual's sense of confidence influences how he or she feels, thinks, is motivated, and behaves. The person's perception—of self, others, and the situation—helps to account for an incredibly wide range of responses: different coping behavior, a variety of stress reactions, the ability to make wise choices, responses to failure, fear of losing control, impact on relationships, new interests, and career pursuits.[63] Enhancing self-confidence, then, is an essential ingredient in any coaching relationship.

---

62 Cited in Gerald Corey, Theory and Practice of Counseling and Psychotherapy, 7th ed., (Belmont, CA: Brooks/Cole-Thomson Learning, 2005), 230.
63 Albert Bandura, "Self-Efficacy Mechanism in Human Agency," American Psychologist 37, no. 2 (1982): 122.

Bandura contends that a person's self-confidence is constructed from four principal sources, including enactive mastery experience, vicarious experience, verbal persuasion, and physiological and emotional states.

1) *Enactive mastery experiences* comprise the number of successes an individual has enjoyed, which produce and reinforce a sense of self-confidence. The positive experiences that produce genuine confidence aren't quick and easy successes but those acquired by overcoming significant obstacles through persistence.

2) *Vicarious experiences* involve observing other people who succeed through sustained effort. Simply by watching others think, plan, and act as they respond to difficult circumstances or open doors of opportunity, the observer is taught effective skills and strategies for dealing with similar experiences.

3) *Verbal persuasion* involves more than conveying positive appraisals of a person's capabilities. It also includes structuring situations for individual success in ways that avoid prematurely placing him or her in risk-filled situations where failure is likely.

4) Lastly, since people rely partly on their bodies and emotions—their *physiological and emotional states*—as they make decisions, it's important to be aware of the impact of exhaustion, elation, worry, anger, and inordinate fear.

In summary, self-confidence is the product of an array of factors. Every aspect of the person's senses is important: intellect, emotions, experiences, relationships, and desire. Those who maintain a strong and resilient sense of confidence set challenging goals and use good analytic thinking, while those with little self-confidence are characterized as being plagued with self-doubts, erratic analytic thinking, and stunted aspirations, resulting in a gradual or sudden deterioration in performance.

Confidence matters. Those who don't believe they can manage the threats they encounter often experience high levels of anxiety and either passivity or frantic action, while those with confidence expend their mental and emotional energies solving the problem.

And confidence breeds more confidence. As a person sees success in tackling a problem or taking advantage of an opportunity, confidence grows. He is then ready to climb an even higher mountain![64] The principle of self-actualizing confidence applies to every area of life: family, work, health, hobbies, and friendships. Certainly, there are limitations each person must face, but those who gain self-confidence can eliminate one barrier to success, growth, and change: their own fears and doubts.

FIVE PROCESSES

Sometimes, change is imposed on us. A spouse calls it quits, our employer changes our job description, or we get an unexpected diagnosis. These and countless other situations demand a response. The kind of change we invite in coaching others, however, is categorically different. We point people to project-focused, self-initiated, intentional change.

In recent years, the Transtheoretical Model (TTM) of therapeutic change was developed by Prochaska and DiClemente. Their model identified five basic *processes* and six *stages* of change.[65] These provide a helpful template as we develop a coaching plan for those we coach and help them achieve their goals.

---

64 Bandura, 115-122, 128-137, 0.2e4 .=x8754262, 279, 329-332.
65 James O. Prochaska and Carlo C. DiClemente, "Transtheoretical Therapy: Toward a More Integrative Model of Change," Psychotherapy: Theory, Research and Practice 19, no. 3 (Fall 1982): 276-278, 285.

The five change processes include: *consciousness raising*, *catharsis*, *choosing*, *conditional stimuli*, and *contingency control*. In these processes, change can be produced at either an experiential or environmental level.

1) In the *consciousness raising* process, the experiential approach is labeled *feedback* (helping people become aware of their internal defenses against change), and the environmental approach is called *education* (information is learned from events). If they aren't aware of the challenges, they won't recognize their choices. They'll continue to be stuck in past habit patterns.

2) *Catharsis* (evoking blocked emotions) on the experiential level is called *corrective emotional experiences*, and the environmental approach is called *dramatic relief*. Many people have wondered for years why they've felt and acted in certain ways—especially self-defeating ways. Surfacing these emotions and habits often brings almost instantaneous insight and relief. People often comment, "Wow, I've been feeling that way for years, but I always thought it was normal."

3) *Choosing* on the experiential level is called *self-liberation* (making a decision from the available responses—action is freely chosen). When changes in the environment lead to more alternatives open to individuals this is a move to *social liberation*. At this point, the person sees new options she never saw before.

4) The *conditional stimuli process* is at the opposite end of changing through choice. In this process, changing an individual's response to stimuli is referred to as *counter-conditioning*, while changing the environment involves *stimulus control procedures*. Many people have deeply entrenched reactions. Now,

they learn to respond to the same people and events in more healthy, positive ways.

5) The final change process is *contingency control*. At this point, the person is *identifying and instituting new contingencies*—rewards and punishments—that govern behavior. These positive and negative consequences reinforce the new habits.

A REVIEW OF THE STAGES OF CHANGE

How does change happen? Experts have studied this topic since the time of the ancient Greeks. In Part 2, we outlined six progressive stages that occur, but may or may not be obvious to those who are watching from the outside. The six stages of change are precontemplation, contemplation, preparation, action, maintenance, and termination. (Experts disagree about the importance of termination as an integral stage. Some argue that termination gives people a clear, final goal on which to focus their attention, but others insist that many—if not most—of the behaviors people want to turn into constructive habits should never end. At DRC, we hold the latter view. For instance, we can't envision any friend or client terminating the new, helpful habits of setting priorities, good planning, exercise, good communication, etc.)

Precontemplation may sound like an odd stage. It's when desires and needs begin to germinate in a person's heart. Without this sense of thirst for something new and different, the person has little motivation to pursue change. The stages follow the logical sequence from thinking to planning to steps of implementation, and finally, to seeing the new behaviors become established habit patterns. Ideally, people progress linearly from one stage to the next. In practice, however, people often experience stalls, regression, and progression, which make the stages more cyclical in nature.

Integration between the processes and stages is important. The verbal processes of change—consciousness raising, catharsis, and choosing—facilitate the stages of contemplation and preparation. Catharsis bridges contemplation and determination, while the behavioral process of contingency control and conditional stimuli are seldom used until the action stage.

CHAPTER 24

RESOLVING CONFLICT

M
any people come to us because they have unresolved tension at work or at home. Their children may be out of control, and they can't find common ground for a solution with their spouse. Or they can't get along with a boss or a coworker. As we'll see, the sources of interpersonal conflict are widely varied, and so is the degree of severity. Conflict is defined by *Merriam-Webster* as "competitive or opposing action of incompatibles: antagonistic state or action (as of divergent ideas, interests, or persons)." Conflict—or the threat of it—has a powerful impact on relationships:

- It clouds thinking.
- It distracts.
- It creates an environment of fear and distrust.
- It makes people reluctant to make decisions.

- It isolates.
- It causes defensive reactions which perpetuate the struggle.

Tension isn't an enemy . . . unless it escalates. Within limits, tension enhances creativity, which leads to better decisions. And because those who disagree have a chance to voice their concerns, they're more likely to support the decision.

We can easily identify the most common "sore spots" in relationships. These include:

- Personality and relationship clashes
- Unspoken and unmet expectations
- Insecurity and identity issues
- Past wounds that make people defensive
- Arrogance and a know-it-all attitude

In companies, churches, nonprofit organizations, and families, Les Parrott III, PhD, identifies 15 Different Types of High-Maintenance Relationships[66]:

1) The Critic: constantly complains and gives unwanted advice
2) The Martyr: forever the victim and wracked with self-pity
3) The Wet Blanket: pessimistic and automatically negative
4) The Steamroller: blindly insensitive to others
5) The Gossip: spreads rumors and leaks secrets
6) The Control Freak: unable to let go and let be
7) The Back-stabber: irrepressibly two-faced
8) The Cold Shoulder: disengages and avoids contact

---

66 Les Parrott III, PhD, High-Maintenance Relationships: How to Handle Impossible People, (Wheaton, IL: Tyndale House, 1996).

9) The Green-Eyed Monster: seethes with envy

10) The Volcano: builds steam and is ready to erupt

11) The Sponge: constantly in need but gives nothing back

12) The Competitor: keeps track of tit for tat

13) The Workhorse: always pushes and is never satisfied

14) The Flirt: imparts innuendoes, which may border on harassment

15) The Chameleon: eager to please and avoids conflict

Not all conflicts have equally destructive power. It's helpful to examine five levels:

LEVEL 1: PREDICAMENTS

In Level 1 conflict, the major objective of the parties is to focus on and solve the problem. No personal attacks here.

LEVEL 2: DISAGREEMENT

In Level 2 conflict, the objective of the parties has shifted slightly; each becomes increasingly concerned about self-protection. Parties are still concerned about solving the problem, but they are especially concerned about coming out of the situation looking good. The language becomes generalized, such as, "I don't know if I can trust our accountant anymore," or "The office manager doesn't seem to be doing his job." These statements leave the hearer wondering what the speaker actually means by the words.

> If you are constantly in conflict with
> people, most likely it is you who have a
> problem. You may be a "conflict carrier."
>
> —JOHN C. MAXWELL

LEVEL 3: CONTEST

At Level 3, conflict has become a full contest. The "players" are less concerned about the problem or looking good; now they want to win, to get their way.

They've lost perspective on the issue. When looking at the larger picture of a conflict at Level 1 or 2, people still see the problem and possible solutions in the foreground. At Level 3, problems and solutions have moved to the background.

- Dichotomizing: Ultimatums, demanding this or that. They demand compliance, and they demand loyalty, for instance, to "our customers" or "my staff." They may make dramatic statements: "If we don't get the money by the end of the month, the company will go under."

- Universalizing: using words like "everybody," "nobody," "never," and "always".

- Magnifications: When we magnify, we assume the other party isn't uninformed—he has evil motives. We also imply that our motives are completely righteous. "At least *I've* given my life to this organization and tried to make this a place where people have a good work ethic!"

■ Fixation on feelings: This means focusing on people's feelings rather than the facts of the problem. "People are unhappy. . . ." "Some people are upset. . . ." "Some are hurt. . . ."

Everything that irritates us about others can lead us to an understanding of ourselves.
—C. G. JUNG

LEVEL 4: FIGHT/FLIGHT/FREEZE

In Level 4, the major objective of parties is to dominate through initiating a fight, running away to avoid the tension, or becoming emotionally paralyzed. No longer is victory palatable. Now the very relationship is a problem. It is an escalation of Level 3, but now parties are naming the "enemy," often not speaking, literally turning their backs, shouting, scowling, and grimacing at one another.

LEVEL 5: INTRACTABLE

At Level 4, the parties were willing to let the other side live, if at a distance. At Level 5, people believe the opposition is so evil that simply getting rid of them will not do. The opposition must be punished or destroyed. Those at Level 5 conflict believe, for the safety of the business, organization, or church, that the bad people must be eliminated or neutralized, so they can do no further damage.

Speak when you are angry and you will
make the best speech you will ever regret.

—AMBROSE BIERCE

FOUR MAJOR PATTERNS FOR CONFLICT MANAGEMENT

Have you noticed that different people respond in a wide variety of ways to relational tension? If we take time to look (and we aren't so traumatized that we can't think clearly), we'll see these patterns. Some people are typically intimidating. That's their way to control people and situations, but others take the opposite strategy: giving in to any perceived demand. Others are more crafty in their desire to dominate. They appear to be compliant, but they say or do things to sabotage the other person. Interestingly, an individual may use one strategy in a certain type of circumstance and a different one in another. Usually, it's a matter of the power differential: those who perceive themselves as superior may exercise power to dominate, but when they face their boss, they're submissive and meek.

Wise, mature people choose over and over again to lay aside any temptation to manipulate others in times of tension. They've learned to speak the truth in a way that other people can hear and respond so that both feel understood.

In your home, office, friendships, and other collections of people, look for these discernable patterns:

1) AGGRESSIVE: "I win; you lose."
2) PASSIVE: "I'll lose; you win."

3) PASSIVE/AGGRESSIVE: "I'll lose, and I'll make sure you do too!"

4) ASSERTIVE: "I win; you win."

KNOWING HOW TO DEFUSE CONFLICT IS A BIG P-L-U-S

Conflicts don't have to be unpleasant. A good question to ask is: "Are we attacking people or problems?" Keep emotions under control by remembering the acronym PLUS.

Pause - Stop whatever else you may be doing and focus on the situation, even if the other person is on the phone.

Listen - Pay attention to what the other person is saying; use body language and paraphrasing to demonstrate you're really listening.

Understand - Make sure you know the real issue and validate the other person's feelings with a response like, "I hear you saying that...."

Solve - Talk about how the two of you might solve the problem. If the solution is your responsibility, tell the other person what you plan to do to resolve the problem and when he or she can expect the matter to be settled.

THE D-E-S-C APPROACH TO EXPRESSING YOURSELF SINCERELY

In relationships that are stressed and conflicted, many of our friends or clients have difficulty formulating thoughts, sorting out emotions, and communicating all of this clearly. When we feel threatened, our brains become overloaded with powerful chemicals, making it very difficult to think clearly. In these times, it's imperative that we slow down, fight through the fog, and follow an effective strategy. I recommend this approach:

DESCRIBE

- Describe the other person's behavior objectively. (Don't describe your emotional response to it.)
- Use concrete terms.
- Describe a specific place, time, and frequency of action.
- Describe the action, not the "motive." (Don't guess at their motives.)

EXPRESS

- Express your feelings and reactions to the other person's behavior.
- Express them calmly—without unleashing an emotional outburst.
- State feelings in a positive manner without putting down or attacking.
- Direct yourself to the offending behavior—not an attack on the character of the person.

STATE

- State specifically what you want.
- Request a small change.
- Ask for only one or two changes.
- Take into account the person's capability to make these changes and their needs.
- Specify what you are willing to do to make the change work.

COOPERATE

- Cooperate to reach a mutually beneficial agreement.
- Don't be embarrassed to talk about rewards and penalties, good consequences and bad consequences, and the "what ifs."
- Allow the other person the freedom to make a commitment.
- Follow up with agreement in writing.

THE RIGHT PRONOUN PREVENTS CONFLICT

The right choice of words is amazingly effective . . . and amazingly simple. When we're in a tense conversation (and when we're preparing for one), we can reframe the conflict by using "I statements" instead of "you statements." For instance:

- REPLACE the blaming "*You* did this" with "Here's what *I* think took place."
- SUBSTITUTE the accusing "*You* shouldn't have done it that way" with "Here's how *I* think it could have been done."
- SUBSTITUTE the aggressive "Why didn't *you* do as you were told?" with "Help *me* understand why what *we* agreed to didn't happen."

No doubt, you will experience some difficult and draining moments as you attempt to lead others. Leadership can be a thankless, lonely, and even discouraging task, simply because you are the one most responsible for the organization. It's very likely you will feel both *affirmed* and *attacked* as you lead people.

Foundational Principles

The ability to resolve (or at least manage) conflict is a skill all of us can acquire. Over the years, I've watched effective leaders and team members, and I've observed some concepts and patterns that have become foundational principles useful in coaching. These include:

1) Often, we must practice the 101% Principle: find the 1% you can agree with, and give it 100% of your attention.

2) When the emotion expressed far outweighs the issue at hand, there is a hidden issue to be faced.

3) In relationships, it is better to build a fence at the top of the cliff than a hospital at the bottom. (Take precautions to lubricate potential trouble.)

4) We must initiate affirmation because most people struggle with insecurity and identity issues.

5) As leaders, we must never place our emotional health in the hands of someone else.

6) Many times our problem is not our problem; it represents only a symptom of a root issue.

7) Hurting people naturally hurt other people.

8) We must embrace the ultimate biblical principle: If I can't get along with people, I can't get along with God.

9) Remember: Conflict is normal. (It is going to happen because we're different.) Conflict is neutral. (It is neither destructive nor constructive in itself.) Conflict is natural. (It's universal; you're not alone in your humanity.)

10) Conflict can be healthy and useful for any organization. It is okay for people to differ with one another. In fact, healthy disagreements often produce the most creative results.

11) Resolutions for the sake of quick agreement are often worse than agreements that are carefully worked out over time.

12) Fair conflict management includes:
- Deal with one issue at a time.
- Clearly define the problem.
- Agree on the problem's definition.
- If more than one issue is presented, agree on the order in which issues will be addressed.
- Explore all the dimensions of the problem(s).
- Explore several alternative solutions to the problem(s).

13) If any party is uncomfortable with the forum in which the conflict is raised, it is legitimate to request and discuss what the most appropriate forum might be.

14) Inappropriate behavior in conflict includes, but isn't limited to:
- Name calling
- Hitting
- Personal attacks
- Talking about people behind their backs
- Mind reading (attributing evil motives to others)
- Inducing guilt ("Look how you've made me feel!")
- Rejecting, deprecating, or discrediting another person
- Using information from confidential sources or indicating such information exists

ACQUIRED SKILLS

As we coach people who are in the middle of tense relationships, we can provide insights, skills, and encouragement they can use throughout the rest of their lives. These pointers have helped countless people:

1) Get to know people and value them, then you can approach the person in conflict personally.

2) If people know you are for them, then when they disagree, they'll still appreciate and respect you.

3) For conflict resolution, a common ground has to be secured; both parties have to trust that the person doesn't have tainted motives.

4) When "motives/intentions" are attached to actions, it gives place to a "root of bitterness." Safeguarding against this will allow you to talk/work things out rationally rather than at the emotional level. Two statements are powerful in lowering the level of heat: "In the middle of our tense conversation, we're still friends and coworkers, not enemies and not right or wrong." And "What is it about our relationship that keeps us from. . . ?"

5) In conflict, we tend to "get big" (leaning forward, raising our voices, glaring) or "get little" (looking down, whispering, not having an opinion). Instead, try to be "even"; not up and down. Don't be easily angered. Don't have a "chip on the shoulder." Be positive.

6) Have your friend or client ask, "Am I a wall builder or a bridge builder?"

7) Pick your battles; don't fight every time you disagree.

8) Don't ignore problems. Anything left on the back burner will burn.

Courage is what it takes to stand up
and speak. Courage is also what it
takes to sit down and listen.

—WINSTON CHURCHILL

WORKABLE STEPS

As long as we are alive and relate to at least one other person, we can count on the fact that there will be conflicts. It's amazing to see young couples preparing for marriage. They're so excited and in love that they can't imagine having an argument or conflict that will shake the romance between them for even a moment. But ask any veteran couple about how they have made their marriage last through the years, and almost always, their reply is that they learned how to overcome conflicts.

Many people will do anything to avoid dealing with conflict. They respond to it by running from it, ignoring it, and avoiding it at all costs, but we must realize that it's natural to have conflict in our lives. The secret to overcoming conflict is in properly reacting to it. Many people respond to virtually any type of conflict in an unhealthy manner. They scream, find fault with the other party involved, refuse to listen to an opinion other than their own, run and hide, and make a scene in front of anyone who may be in the room.

Although conflict is never a comfortable or pleasant experience, it can be dealt with in a manner that will bring about more positive results. It all begins with taking the focus off of ourselves and thinking of the other person involved, whether it is a coworker, employer, employee, friend, or family member. If conflict is approached with the goal to prove ourselves right, the end result will be damaging to the relationship.

The first step to take in order to bring resolve to a conflict is putting yourself in the other person's shoes. By gaining perspective on how *they* feel in the situation, it will help to defuse your own anger, taking the focus off your personal emotions. In order to accomplish this, you must listen more than you speak. When you listen, you have to avoid *reading into* what they are saying and distorting it, making it worse than it already is.

Also, don't interrupt by interjecting your thoughts as they express themselves. Interruptions only add to the intensity of the conflict and break down the communication even further. Listening intently and showing genuine concern for the other person's feelings will provide a much calmer atmosphere and will allow resolution to take place between you.

Be willing to apologize and take responsibility for your part in the conflict. (After all, it does take two to tango.) At the end of the day, does it really matter if you're proven to be right? Even when you don't feel you're in the wrong, if you take the initiative to bring resolution to the conflict, you really do *win* because you will free yourself from the stress of having to walk away as the "victor" in the situation. We all know it's hard to argue with a person who won't fight back. Remember that a soft answer turns away wrath!

Never scream and insult the person during a conflict. Abusive language and behavior never get you anywhere and only show immaturity and selfishness. When you allow your emotions to get to this point, it produces more destruction. If you find yourself at the "boiling point" and you can no longer control yourself, you need to walk away to avoid doing or saying anything that you can't undo or unsay. Take the time to gather your composure and control of your thoughts before continuing the conversation. If the conflict is going to be resolved and the relationship strengthened, someone has to be the "bigger person." It may as well be you! The power of life and death surely does lie in our tongues.

CHAPTER 25

FINANCIAL FREEDOM

People may have very different ways to identify and describe what they mean by "financial freedom." For many, it's getting out from under the crushing burden of debt. For a number of reasons, they're drowning in red ink, and they don't know how to swim! Others feel comfortable and free as long as they can look at their checkbook balance at the end of the month and see a little bit more than when the month started. They want help managing their expenses to be sure they don't surpass their income. And still others have an eye on the future—college for their children, vacations, a second home, or retirement. They want a coach's help to point them in the right direction.

To be prepared for the range of needs and desires, we need to explore the causes of financial problems in the lives of those we coach, including their relationships with money, and some basic principles of budgeting, spending, saving, and investing. Of course, most of us aren't trained or certified to be financial planners, so we need to refer people to someone who can help them with their investments. Our role is to focus on getting them to a place where investing is even a possibility.

COMMON FINANCIAL PROBLEMS

We could probably list dozens of red-flag and yellow-flag issues that create problems for people in their financial lives, but let's focus on those that are most common:

Excessive Spending

This is the number one culprit. Many people lack impulse control, so they buy things they don't need. They come up with elaborate excuses to justify each purchase, and they often insist, "This is the last thing I'm going to buy for a long time," but the cumulative effect is that they run in the red every month . . . and they don't have substantive, effective plans to get to black.

Excessive Borrowing

This is the almost inevitable corollary to the spending problem. It's too easy for people to charge purchases on credit cards and pay only the minimum monthly charge. The interest is usually in double digits, so even the minimum charge can be a stretch for many of them. By making only this payment, they don't make a dent in the balance of the debt. Paying only the minimum affects the borrower's credit score, which causes them to pay higher interest rates, exacerbating the problem.

Insisting on New Cars

As soon as you drive a new car off the lot, you're taking an immediate and significant financial hit. Depreciation begins in the parking lot. Used cars are often a much better deal, even if they're not as prestigious or thrilling.

Too Much House

This was a huge problem in the collapse of the housing bubble in 2007-2009, and many people were hurt when the values of their homes went below their loan amounts—they were "upside down." It can still be a problem today. The temptation of historically low interest rates and rising home values make many buyers eager to jump in, but they often have short memories about the downturns that inevitably occur in economic cycles.

Student Loan Debt

The most recent survey shows that 69% of college students have taken student loans, with the average graduate owing almost $30,000. This has become one of the biggest financial drags on young people. It was easy for students to get these loans, but they're finding it difficult to pay off the significant debt they incurred. And many of them aren't making as much as they would if they'd gone to a trade school.

Bad Business Decisions

A man with a very good job as the office manager at a law firm had always wanted to own his own business. He left his job and bought a steel fabricating company. He thought it was a dream come true, but he knew very little about the industry. In less than two years, his company went bankrupt. He now works as an office manager at a different law firm, but he's out several hundred thousand dollars. Two of the problems for dreamers are making assumptions about how easy it will be to make a lot of money and the failure to get sound advice from knowledgeable people—or not listening when they get it.

Economic Downturns

The economy goes in cycles. Economists have very sophisticated models to predict the next phase, but whether they're right or wrong, most people assume things will always move upward. They don't. The banking and housing crisis of 2007-2009 and the COVID pandemic in 2020-2021 caused millions to lose their jobs and go into debt. We're wise to make financial decisions—about expenses, income, or investments—with a realistic perspective and save at least six months' worth of income as a cushion against unforeseen financial problems.

Medical Expenses

A man who had outpatient surgery was devastated when he got a bill for over $220,000. A trip to the emergency room, cancer treatment, or any other major medical procedure can wreck a family's finances. Insurance may seem like a luxury to many who are young, but it's essential for all of us.

Divorce Complications

Many couples stay in their loveless marriages for the financial stability, or they divorce to get away without thinking clearly about the settlement. Without this security, they can find themselves emotionally devastated and without means of support.

Differing Values and Desires

In marriage, opposites attract, but they can also create conflict over their views of budgeting, spending, and investing. In fact, it usually takes considerable effort to wade into these conversations, so both spouses feel understood, are willing to compromise, and negotiate a plan and budget—and then resolve disputes when one or both of them don't follow the plan.

RELATING TO MONEY

It may seem strange to think of a person's "relationship to money," but it's helpful to see that we treat money like we treat things or people. Some of us view money like a tank of gas, to be used and filled up again whenever we need it. Others see it as someone to party with, and the highest and best use of money is to pay for a good time. Some view money as a trusted friend, something to value and nurture, and others as a security blanket to keep one safe and warm. Our relationships to people are shaped to a great degree by our past relationships, especially when we were children.

In the same way, our perceptions of money have been shaped by events that happened when we were young. Financial planner Jim Munchbach, the author of *Make Your Money Count*, begins his relationships with prospective clients by asking two questions. First, "What are some of your early memories about money?" After they think about it and answer, he asks a second question: "What are some ways those experiences affect your attitudes and choices about money today?" They may share something about the importance of their allowance, how they earned money for the first time, or how their parents were ashamed of being in debt. He reports, "I've been amazed at some of the stories people have told me, and I've also been amazed at their insights about the life-changing impact of these experiences."[67] Munchbach writes that these questions are especially insightful for those who struggle with debt because they can then identify the source of their faulty thinking and misplaced desires. Quite often, a person's relationship to money is a reflection—the same or the opposite reflection—of one of the parents.

As we talk with our friends and clients, we can consider asking Jim Munchbach's two questions to uncover long-buried but very powerful perceptions of the meaning of money.

THE PURPOSE OF MONEY

Money is never just money—it means far more than just numbers in an account or on a bill. People use money for a wide range of purposes, but it's always a means, not an end. Let's examine the most common purposes. These overlap and interlock, but you'll see the distinctions.

Pleasure

As we've seen, some use money for pleasure. Money is the door to fun, ease, and excitement. People who have this purpose for money daydream about the next party, the next vacation, the newest tech device, or the next purchase for entertainment, like the latest and biggest television or sound system.

Power

Wealth is associated with power, and poverty and debt with powerlessness. When we have money, we can do things others can't, we

---

67 Jim Munchbach, Make Your Money Count (Friendswood, TX: Baxter Press, 2007), 50.

impress people, and we can go into places of authority that are closed to people without means.

Control

Control is similar to power, but it's different. We may use money to control our sense of security, our future, people's opinions of us, and our sense of well-being.

Approval

It's human nature; we think more highly of people who "have made it" than those who haven't. Money buys things that impress people, and that feels really good.

These purposes are standard equipment in the hearts of people, and there's nothing inherently wrong with pleasure, power, control, or approval . . . unless one or more of these becomes our consuming passion. We function better and we experience more fulfillment when we get off the endless wheel of comparison and competition and find meaning beyond self-indulgence. People are more important than all these things. In a commencement address at Kenyon College, novelist David Foster Wallace put his finger on the problem with making secondary things primary:

> *If you worship money and things—if they are where you tap real meaning in life—then you will never have enough. Never feel you have enough. It's the truth. Worship your own body and beauty and sexual allure and you will always feel ugly, and when time and age start showing, you will die a million deaths before they finally plant you. On one level, we all know this stuff already—it's been codified as myths, proverbs, clichés, bromides,*

epigrams, parables: the skeleton of every great story. The trick is keeping the truth up front in daily consciousness. Worship power—you will feel weak and afraid, and you will need ever more power over others to keep the fear at bay. Worship your intellect, being seen as smart—you will end up feeling stupid, a fraud, always on the verge of being found out.[68]

As coaches, it's important for us to address the obvious issues of budgeting, but to make a lasting impact, we should take time to uncover others' true perceptions of the meaning of money.

BUDGETING

Whether people are multimillionaires or being swallowed in debt, most people could use some help crafting a better budget—and often, having one at all! The necessary process of identifying expenses is tedious, but our friends and clients may not get far without this exercise, and some will need to make some fairly drastic decisions. Popular author and radio host Dave Ramsey recommends people in debt learn to live on "beans and rice, rice and beans" until they're out of debt. Those we coach may benefit from debt consolidation services, so a referral may be welcome.

Instead of asking people to work up a list of arbitrary expenses, have them look at their checks, recurring charges to their account, and credit card charges from the last week or two. These are actual expenses. If they insist that one or more was unusual, ask how often they have unusual expenses, and factor that in.

---

68 "This Is Water," David Foster Wallace, Kenyon College, www.theguardian.com/books/2008/sep/20/fiction.

They can use a chart like this, and remind them to include absolutely everything.

DATE	ITEM	AMOUNT
Monday		
Tuesday		
Wednesday		
Thursday		
Friday		
Saturday		
Sunday		

It may help to complete this exercise for a month to be sure everything is listed.

SAVING AND INVESTING

A report shows that 40% of Americans would struggle to come up with $400 to pay for an unexpected expense.[69] They live paycheck to paycheck, and they have nothing left at the end of the month—no extra cash in hand, no savings, no cushion, no peace of mind.

As we've seen, an economic downturn can cause a loss of income, or medical expenses or out-of-control spending may be the cause of a financial problem. In some cases, finding a job is the most immediate goal, followed by self-imposed austerity and debt relief. At some point, however, everyone needs to have a viable goal of saving and investing. Certainly, many people insist, "It's too late for me. I've missed the window." It's true that they should have started earlier, but it's never too late to start. A reasonable savings goal is an essential element of financial freedom. As this number grows, people can consider more sophisticated investments. At that point, their needs are beyond the scope of our expertise, so we can refer them to a financial advisor with a strong track record and a sterling reputation.

As always, as we work with people with any kind of need or desire, instilling hope is perhaps our greatest service to them. Debt crushes the spirit and consumes thoughts, creating nagging doubts and anxiety. Those we coach need to know that a new day is dawning. It'll take courage and tenacity to make progress and reach their goals, but you're there to help them take steps along the way.

---

69 Cited in the "2018 Survey of Household Economics and Decision Making."

CHAPTER 26

CHARTING A CAREER TRAJECTORY

I n coaching people about their careers, the most frequent comment is, "I hate this job! But I feel stuck with no way out. Can you help me?"

Yes, yes, we can, and hopefully, our friends will gain much more than a new business card after our coaching relationship ends.

Some people come to us with misplaced expectations. They may assume helping them write a killer resume is the limit of our expertise, or they may expect us to serve as headhunters and find the perfect job for them, or they may have already concluded that one session with us will give them all the direction they could ever need. It's important, then, for us to do a thorough intake and determine if any of these misconceptions (or any others) threaten to adversely affect the relationship.

TWO POINTS OF CHANGE

People seek our help at primarily two points in their careers: when they're seeking a promotion and when they're transitioning out of one company and into another. They often admit they feel stuck and confused. They've wanted to kick their careers into another gear for a long time, but they haven't been able to make it happen.

When someone is looking at the next rung up the ladder in their organization, we might begin by asking:

- "What do you find fulfilling in your current role?"
- "What's frustrating, boring, or not a good fit for you in this position?"
- "Describe the role that you think fits you best."
- "Are you looking for the next step up in what you're doing now, or are you considering a very different role in a different part of the organization?"
- "Tell me about your most recent performance review. Do you think it was accurate? Why or why not?"
- "How would you describe the payoffs and challenges of the promotion?"

If the person is considering a transition out of the company, you may want to ask:

- "What's compelling your decision to leave?"
- "Who, if anyone, is recommending that you leave the company and find a career somewhere else?"
- "If you could change your current situation, what changes would you make?"
- "Describe the role you envision somewhere else."

- "Have you applied for other positions? If you have, what response did you get?"
- "How would you describe the payoffs, losses, and challenges of this move?"

Of course, ask follow-up questions to clarify the person's thinking and get beneath the surface. Some people are ambitious for advancement. They want their names on C-suite doors, and they'll do anything to get there. Others want (or need) to make more money to pay for their children's college costs, care for an elderly parent, or pad their retirement accounts. But many people are simply looking for a better fit—a role that aligns their career with their values, interests, and skills. For them, the cultural factors of the company values and relationships are more important than new titles or raises. When you determine the underlying motivations, you'll be able to target your questions to stimulate further self-discovery.

WHEN PEOPLE NEED A COACH

Certainly, employees and executives can benefit from professional coaching at any point in their careers, but we find it to be most helpful at particular tension points:

Just out of College

Students have spent years preparing for their careers, but many of them don't really know what it's like to "work in the real world." Internships have become useful for the interns and the companies to have a "test run" to gauge the fit. Still, employers and their HR departments would be wise to offer coaching services to newly graduated employees to help them make the transition from running their own schedules in college to being disciplined, effective employees in the company.

A New, Bold Vision for Advancement

Those who are go-getters can use a coach's expertise to help them target and achieve the next step in their advancement. Sometimes, these people are a delight to their bosses because they're overachievers, but they may be perceived by their peers (the very people they hope to lead) as overbearing and rude. Our task is to celebrate their vision and help them relate up the chain of command and to their peers with a measure of kindness and understanding.

Stuck . . . Just Stuck

In many cases, the people who come to us feel like they've hit a dead end. They've been doing the same thing for so long—too long—and they want to do something else. The problem is that they haven't developed the skills to move up, and they may not have the flexibility to leave the company and find a job somewhere else. Our role is to instill a sense of hope and newfound confidence. Seldom is anyone really at a dead end. There are almost always more options than they've considered, and even if they stay in their current role, we can help them experience more fulfillment, establish reasonable expectations, and build better relationships with their bosses and coworkers.

ASSESSMENTS

Coaches have a wide array of resources to help people with their career trajectory. We can use personality inventories, skills assessments, interest inventories, and other tools. One of the most helpful is a 360 assessment. Input from family members, colleagues, bosses, and those who report to the friend or client are asked to give frank comments. These are confidential and sent directly to the coach, who then evaluates them, eliminates outliers (or explores them more fully), and gives a report to the person.

BEYOND YOU

When we coach people who come with any kind of need, we invite them to be forthright and vulnerable with us as they learn that we're trustworthy. In this process, the angst a person feels in a dead-end job may be far more severe than it appeared in the first session. We may learn the person is suffering from panic attacks, chronic anxiety, or depression. Their approach-avoidance in the first few sessions signaled they desperately wanted help but were afraid to take any steps of change, maybe blaming us for pushing too hard when we were, in fact, very gentle and deferential. Don't try to be a psychiatrist. Perhaps the best thing we can do for them is refer them to a doctor for an assessment. Usually, the first stop is their own physician, who can refer to a specialist if necessary.

LOOK FOR . . .

As always, we're looking for those who are engaged in self-discovery and eager to take steps forward. In an article in *Forbes*, a career coach described her "dream client":

> *Someone who is open to new ideas, willing to step out of his or her comfort zone and motivated to embark on the work that makes up the job-search-and-career-change process. What's more, a good client allows the coach to be a partner in that process. It's actually essential because there are so many tricky*

*steps along the way, whether it's the tough job market or a very
lengthy career change. So clients should reach out for as much
help as possible—from the coach and from everyone else in their
personal or professional networks—in order to succeed.*[70]

It is our privilege and pleasure to help people find the right career
fit—if not for the rest of their lives, at least for the next important season.

COACHING TOP LEADERS

JEFF SCOTT SMITH

President, JSS Consulting; Master Coach Trainer, Dream Releaser Coaching

Companies used to hire executive coaches to rescue underperforming executives. Today, however, most companies hire executive coaches to invest in their top executives and emerging leaders. Coaching no longer carries a negative connotation. Now, it's a status symbol.

Executives function in environments that present staggering demands. The pressure of leading people in today's complex, competitive global marketplace is exhausting. Therefore, the opportunity to have a professional coach is often seen as a significant benefit, a perk of the job. It indicates that an organization sees the executive as promising and worth the investment.

---

70 Demetrius Cheeks, "About Career Coaching," Forbes, https://www.forbes.com/sites/learnvest/2013/07/09/10-things-you-should-know-about-career-coaching/?sh=2d9f01f47d5e.

WHAT IS EXECUTIVE COACHING?

Executive coaching is defined as the relationship between a client who has managerial authority and responsibility in an organization and a coach who uses a variety of techniques to aid the client in reaching mutually agreed upon goals. The focus is to improve the professional performance and personal fulfillment of the executive. This improvement will consequently enhance the effectiveness of the executive's organization. Coach and client formally define this relationship so that goals and expectations are clearly defined.

Although many coaches have a consulting or therapeutic background, they refrain from giving advice or solving their clients' problems for them. The focus is on self-discovery, and it focuses on ways to move forward instead of processing the past.

WHERE DO MOST EXECUTIVE LEVEL CLIENTS NEED HELP?

Six areas that consistently rank at the top of the client's needs include the following:

1) **Self-Awareness**. This area is defined as a thorough understanding of one's essential characteristics including qualities, needs, values, strengths, weaknesses, being, and identity. Through coaching, a client can improve the range, flexibility, and effectiveness of their behavioral repertoire.

2) **Impact and Influence**. This involves leadership presence, and it requires knowing how to inspire people and build momentum in an organization. Coaching helps a client become a great leader because he or she learns how to inspire respect, admiration, and hard work from others. Different skill sets need to be learned to effectively manage down, manage across, and manage up.

3) **Goal setting**. This is about meeting objectives. A goal must have a deadline and be specific, measurable, and compelling. Through coaching, clients can learn how their thoughts affect their moods, how those moods affect their behaviors, and how those behaviors ultimately affect goal setting and help drive results, both professionally and personally.

4) **Targeted Performance Area**. Executive coaching can help the client manage a particular area that they recognize they need to work on, such as anger management, trust building, decision-making, staffing, and many other executive functions. In addition, a coach can assist with the improvement of the executive's overall effectiveness in the management of the organization or team.

5) **Situational Leadership**. This is learning how to address whatever scenarios happen to come up during the day with the right leadership style for the person or situation at hand. One must be able to adapt to lead in different ways for different circumstances. Coaching can assist in developing the ability to manage self and others in various scenarios, especially during times of crisis, conflict, and change.

6) **Life Management**. Balancing the multifaceted demands on executives can present challenges. Through coaching, clients can improve their ability to manage tensions between organization, community, and personal needs.

EXECUTIVE COACHING PROCESS

Step 1: Establish Coaching Agreement

Executive coaching involves active communication between the coach, the executive, and the stakeholders. Therefore, the terms of the coaching contract and guidelines are agreed upon at the very beginning. Two things happen at this point:

- Commitment must be established from the organization and from the person who will be coached so that clear guidelines are understood.
- The importance of confidentiality in the coaching relationship is discussed. The information shared between coach and client is to remain private. The coach will sign a confidentiality agreement.

Step 2: Determine Key Stakeholders

The stakeholders are identified and ongoing support for the coaching program is clearly agreed upon. The key stakeholders can come from the Human Resources Department, senior management, the participant's immediate manager, or a sponsor.

Step 3: Collect Assessment Data and Feedback

Information gathering involves collecting feedback from the client, sponsors, 360-degree data, and performance reviews. This comprehensive process helps the coach design a developmental plan that is customized for that particular executive.

Step 4: Identify Coaching Objectives

Identify the most important objectives and specific performance goals for the coaching relationship. A measurable action plan is developed, identifying the key behaviors to be changed and outlining specific metrics to be achieved. Designing objectives and metrics at this stage assures that the benefits are clearly achieved and the return on investment is known.

Step 5: Implement Action Plan

This stage implements the required actions and behavior changes, so the desired results are achieved. Coach, client, and stakeholders are all involved in this process.

Step 6: Provide Progressive Review and Feedback

A monthly informal review of the coaching process is conducted. The coaching participant meets with his/her manager to share progress and gain feedback.

Step 7: Deliver Post-Coaching Follow-Up

At the end of the coaching engagement, a review of the entire process takes place. After the last session, the key stakeholders, immediate boss, and human resources will participate in a close-out meeting. They will review the success achieved, create a future action plan, and identify the type of support and resources necessary to continue the executive's development.

COACHING AND CONSULTING

Coaching and consulting can easily become intertwined. Both develop a helping relationship with the client, but a number of factors determine if this relationship becomes coaching or consulting. First, who initiated the process, the client or the client's boss? Second, who determines the coaching goal and the desired outcome, the client or the client's boss? Third, is the client working on an individual or organizational issue? Fourth, what is the status difference between the coach and client? In each of these scenarios the coach may need to assess what is required in the moment and move in and out of both coaching and consultant roles.

CHAPTER 27

LEADING THROUGH CHAOS

CASE STUDY

Richard had been working in sales for a major pharmaceutical company, but when he was offered a senior position with a new hospital corporation, he jumped at the opportunity. The first six months were wonderful. He led his department skillfully, and the team enjoyed working together. They contributed to the company's success in a major way. Every day, Richard was grateful that the job was such a good fit.

When the CEO hired a marketing director, Richard was told the new guy was something special. He soon found out that "special" could have more than one meaning. Jonathan was bold and brash, and he took offense at anything anyone said, including Richard. When Richard tried to build a relationship with him by taking him out to lunch, they had a pleasant conversation, but the next day, someone told Richard that Jonathan had spread rumors that Richard had tried to form an alliance with him against the CEO. And the CEO had heard those rumors too.

Richard immediately called for a meeting with Jonathan and the CEO to "clear the air." Somehow, Jonathan had convinced the CEO that Richard had, in fact, tried to undermine his leadership. The CEO demanded an apology and a promise that Richard wouldn't continue his subterfuge. Needless to say, this wasn't the kind of resolution Richard was looking for!

The problem was that this was only the first chapter in a very long book of episodes when Richard was caught in the middle between a scheming peer and a boss who couldn't decide whom to believe, but seemed to always side with Jonathan because Jonathan communicated with more certainty and forcefulness, and marketing was the lifeline of the company.

Richard tried numerous times to cut through the craziness, speak honestly, and keep an open mind, but after three years of power plays and disappointments, Richard decided to leave the company. It was a bitter pill to swallow, one that wasn't made any sweeter when it was discovered that Jonathan had been embezzling funds from his company account and was fired a few months after Richard left.

Through all of this, one friend in the company was Richard's lifeline to sanity. William was in Richard's department, and early in the saga, he became a trusted resource to let Richard vent his frustration and be a sounding board for him. "Those three years were really hard," Richard told William on the day he packed up his office, "but it would have been hell without your friendship."

Sooner or later, every leader hits a wall, gets stuck in the mud, or faces a tsunami of criticism. Whatever metaphor you think fits best, it's chaos. One of the tests of leadership, and of those aspiring to higher levels of leadership, is the ability to navigate through these turbulent times.

PLANNED CHAOS

It's easy to identify two distinct sources of organizational disruption: planned and unplanned. Leaders plan to disrupt the system when they make major changes to the organizational reporting system, merge with other companies, or create new product lines. These leaders have the luxury of planning for the chaos well before it happens, anticipating how people will respond (especially particular people), and starting the process of calming nerves and assuring people of their places long before the memo goes out.

At the beginning of the twentieth century, the South Pole hadn't been explored. A couple of expeditions set off to find the pole. One of those was led by the British explorer Ernest Shackleton. He planned to sail as close to the pole as possible and then trek over the ice and out again on the far side of the continent. He was under no illusions about what the endeavor would demand from the men who joined him. He ran this ad in a London newspaper:

"Men wanted for hazardous journey. Low wages, bitter cold, long hours of complete darkness. Safe return doubtful. Honor and recognition in event of success."

The men who responded to the ad were prepared for the dangers, so they showed remarkable courage and good spirits. Over two long years, they faced adversity after adversity: Their ship got stuck in the ice and was slowly crushed by the floe. The men had to camp on the shifting ice for more than a year until they made a daring escape in small boats to a remote island off the shore of the continent. From there, Shackleton and five other men set out in a small boat in one-hundred-foot seas and howling winds to find the whaling port of South Georgia, a dot of an island eight hundred miles away. For sixteen days, they navigated one of the little boats through furious winds and one-hundred-foot waves.

Later, Shackleton remembered, "Every surge of the sea was an enemy to be watched and circumvented. The wind simply shrieked as it tore the tops off the waves. Down into the valleys, up to tossing heights, straining until her seams opened, swung our little boat." When they found it, they couldn't get to the port on the other side because of the storms, so they climbed a mountain ridge and hiked into the village. When they arrived, "Their hair and beards stringy and matted, their faces blackened with soot from blubber stoves and creased from nearly two years of stress and privation."

A whaler gazed at the men who had come from the no-man's-land of the mountains behind the port and asked, "Who the hell are you?"

The soot and grime covered them, and the man in the middle said, "My name is Shackleton."

The whaler was moved to tears. He had heard that everyone in the expedition had died in the cold, but here was the leader of the team—exhausted but courageous.[71]

---

71 "The Stunning Survival Story of Ernest Shackleton and His Endurance Crew," Frank Hurley, History, https://www.history.com/news/shackleton-endurance-survival.

This was planned chaos. Through it all, not a man was lost, even though they faced unimaginable cold, darkness, and the danger of being crushed by ice or eaten by enormous leopard seals. They failed in their goal of reaching the pole, but they succeeded in becoming the stuff of legends.

When we assist a leader who is making decisions that will cause chaos in the organization, we need to follow the example of Ernest Shackleton:

1) Build a great team.
2) Create a culture of vision and trust.
3) Prepare for the change.
4) Keep injecting optimism and confidence into your people.

Every company has two organizational structures: The formal one is written on the charts; the other is the everyday relationship of the men and women in the organization.
—HAROLD S. GENEEN, FORMER CHAIRMAN, ITT

UNPLANNED CHAOS

Far more often, disruption happens seemingly out of the blue. Leaders have carefully crafted plans and taken bold steps, but something unforeseen happens that throws everything out of balance. The problem is bad enough, but the frantic reaction of the people involved multiplies the stress and uncertainty. In these situations, leaders can quickly feel overwhelmed. When they call us for help, we can offer a calm, steady hand to help them right the ship. Our assistance often involves these elements:

- **An accurate assessment:** One of the most helpful roles we play as coaches is to help the leader determine responsibility and authority. These overlap, but they're not identical. Responsibilities are the duties of each person involved, and authority is the power to give directives to others. A careful analysis of the people, the situation, and how the situation developed usually surfaces important information that will guide decisions in the near future. In this review, you'll identify who did what, why they did it, how they did it, and how others responded.

- **Back to basics:** Leaders can do a lot to ease anxiety in themselves and others by clarifying (or stating for the first time) the basic values of the organization: Who are we? Why do we exist? How do we operate? What impact do we have on each other and others? This isn't a fill-in-the-blank exercise. As we enter the fray to coach the leader, we might accurately assume that one of the causes of the chaos is the lack of clear and compelling organizational values. It's important to take time to focus on these at this point in the process—and communicate them clearly and often as the process unfolds.

- **Develop a plan:** The plan needs to include the steps toward sanity and profitability, the responsibilities of each person, the authority to make decisions, the communication of the steps, the timeline, and the payoff for the organization and each person.

- **Make positive assumptions about people:** A common problem during chaotic times is that people become suspicious of each other. They form informal but powerful alliances, and anyone who is outside of the alliance is considered nothing more than an evil fool. Too harsh? Just listen to how people talk about each other. It's toxic and destructive. The leader's role is to bring honesty and kindness into the conversation, not one or the other. When we believe the people who disagree with us deserve respect, we'll treat them with honor and patience. The leader's example goes a long way to bring calm and conciliation back to the team.

- **Prepare for pushback:** No matter how clearly leaders communicate, and no matter how calmly and positively they speak, some people on the team won't like what they hear. They may be predisposed to disagree, or they may not like some of the particulars of the plan. Either way, the leader needs to be ready with a clear script to speak to those who aren't on board yet.

- **Lean on your allies:** This may sound like the building of alliances I just warned against, but leaders need to know whom they can count on as they roll out the plan and make the necessary adjustments to the organizational chart and schedule. Those who support the leader don't have to be loud about it. They may work quietly behind the scenes to offer words of optimism and confidence to those who are still upset or suspicious.

- **Make hard choices:** In times of chaos, it's almost certain that some difficult decisions need to be made. Someone may need to be moved to a role that's more suitable to his or her skills, and someone else may need to be terminated. This is perhaps the most explosive time in the process of turning chaos into progress. Your friend or client needs to work closely with HR to be sure everything is buttoned up and nailed down before these conversations happen.

■ **Through it all, stay positive:** People in the organization feed off the mood of the leader. If the leader is unsure, they'll lose confidence. If they believe the leader is blowing smoke (that is, being duplicitous), they'll be suspicious. But if they sense the leader has a strong sense of hope that things are going to work out, they'll be more willing to be flexible and work hard to make the solution a success.

SENSEMAKING

Scholars at the Sloan School of Management at MIT have identified a key trait that leaders need during times of chaos. In an article titled "The Overlooked Key to Leading Through Chaos," they call it *sensemaking*, which "involves pulling together disparate views to create a plausible understanding of the complexity around us and then testing that understanding to refine it or, if necessary, abandon it and start over. . . . It is considered essential for innovation and crucial to the development of nimble teams and organizations." This process moves past the assumptions that the world will work the way it always has, and instead, it makes the opposite assumption: "Rather than immediately jumping to solutions, we must start with collecting data and scrutinizing it for trends and patterns that point to better solutions; rather than ignoring warning signs of failure, we should learn from others what those warning signs might be. This is not the time to do less sensemaking—it is the time to supercharge your organization's ability to do more."[72]

In many ways, a coach's role in assisting leaders who are experiencing organizational chaos is helping them make sense of things. We don't look for quick answers to a complex web of problems. We carefully and hopefully walk with the leader to uncover the root cause, craft a clear plan, and do the sticky but necessary work of implementing the plan.

AVOIDING CHAOS

One of the most important tasks of a leader is selecting and developing a team. If an organization is struggling but the team is functioning well, they have hope, and they feed off each other's encouragement. But even when a business is making a lot of money or a nonprofit is growing, a sour team environment poisons the atmosphere like acidic smog.

Having the right people on the team is another crucial factor in the health and effectiveness of a team. Selection is critical. It's much easier to train someone who has enthusiasm and skills than spending months (or years) trying to bring a lethargic or resistant person up to speed.

Proper people placement prevents (or at least limits) problems. People have many different motives, and they experience a wide variety of circumstances that might prompt them to offer themselves for a position. Don't limit your search to those who offer to fill a spot. Even if someone seems to fit, slow down the process to look thoroughly for the very best person to fill the position.

Four essentials for choosing a team are character (integrity, honesty, trustworthiness), competency (skilled and timely), chemistry (a good

72 "The Overlooked Key to Leading Through Chaos," Deborah Ancona, Michele Williams, and Gisela Gerlach, MIT Sloan Management Review, September 8, 2020, https://sloanreview.mit.edu/article/the-overlooked-key-to-leading-through-chaos/.

fit with others on the team), and courage (the willingness to speak up and take bold action when it's required).

After a team is recruited, spend time learning about them as individuals. Specifically, look at these four A's:

1) Attitudes

Discover who they are by understanding their attitude toward their job and the people around them.

2) Affinities

What do they like? Whom do they like? Knowing alliances are still there can help current leaders to make a smooth transition.

3) Anxieties

What causes them stress? If a particular executive creates stress among employees, running interference can enable them to concentrate on their job.

4) Animosities

What is it and whom is it they don't like? A simple change could make them happier.

Leaders can only react to information if first they know about it. Take time to get to know your players.

COACHING: THE KEY TO TRANSFORMATIONAL LEADERSHIP

NICHOLAS JOHN
CEO of LeaderGrow

What does coaching have to do with leadership? Everything! We have often separated the disciplines of coaching and leadership, but coaching is an integral part in the development of leaders. Actually, coaching in its purest form is the basis for the sustainable development of leaders. In today's global corporate environment, employers need to have the benefit of coaching for their employees, while at the same time increasing their organizational capacity by developing these employees to become the next generation of leaders. Therefore, instead of coaching individual leaders to improve their own performance, coaching skills are leveraged to create a transformational leadership style where the client eventually becomes the coach, and thereby, multiplies transformational leadership through the art of coaching.

The concept of transformational leadership through the art of coaching is the basis for the tested methodology in our organization. This methodology is simple yet effective in unearthing a pool of leadership talent that will ensure the continued and sustainable success of any organization.

This diagram illustrates the key steps, demonstrating the significance of coaching as an overall part of the leadership journey for sustainable transformational leadership in an organization.

DIAGRAM—THE LEADERSHIP JOURNEY

Let me share a more detailed explanation of this methodology:

1) Identify Emerging Leaders

In the beginning of the process, an organization selects their next generation of emerging leaders by reviewing:

- Who are their most talented employees?
- Which employees are part of their leadership succession planning?
- Who has the leadership potential that can be developed for the future of the organization?

2) Leadership Development

The emerging leaders are put onto a focused leadership development program to harness their potential and abilities. Our program is called PILOT (Preparing Integral Leaders of Tomorrow). PILOT is a foundational leadership program designed to equip and empower emerging leaders with the building blocks that will remain relevant throughout their leadership journey. (Many organizations have their own in-house or outsourced leadership development programs.)

3) Coaching

In this step, coaching becomes an integral part of the journey for future leaders. During step two, leadership development, many emerging leaders require individual attention in one or several areas. It is our experience that a large percentage of individuals that complete our PILOT program require a more personal support structure in a general or specific area of their lives. For example:

- Some individuals may require additional development in specific leadership blocks covered in the PILOT program.
- Some individuals may be stuck in an area of their professional or personal lives and have not been able to make needed changes.
- Some individuals may require attention in their personal growth and development.

Here, personalized coaching is an essential step in the continued development of emerging leaders. It involves critical analysis, thinking, and exploration that will build a foundation for effective action for these emerging leaders.

4) Becoming a Coach

Finally, some of the leaders who experience the benefits of leadership development combined with personalized coaching (which before may have seemed mutually exclusive elements) are inspired and want to play a part in transforming the lives of others in the organisation. In this way, the leadership journey comes full circle and continues to expand. Multiplying transformational leadership should be the ultimate goal for every organization.

The two most significant benefits of such an approach are that:

1) It helps to increase your leadership pool:

   Organizational Capacity

2) It helps to increase your customer base:

   Customer Satisfaction

The methodology of transformational leadership and coaching is proven to increase an organization's leadership pool, while also retaining present customers. It will also enhance your organizational capacity and attract top-notch leaders who want to take the leadership journey.

Coaching is pivotal to the sustainable development of leaders. Coaching and a transformational leadership program can create a unique and sustainable advantage for any organization.

So ... what does coaching have to do with leadership? Everything!

ABOUT LEADERGROW

LeaderGrow exists to help develop the leadership potential and grow the leadership capability of talented young individuals within organizations today. We take what is in their hearts and equip them for self-leadership and the leadership of others within their family, their community, and ultimately their organization.

We are focused on the creation and facilitation of **quality, integrous, and purpose-driven leaders,** so that collectively we can contribute to the development of a strong culture of leadership within organizations globally.

We help people become leaders. We provide individuals with the training, encouragement, and coaching to become inspirational leaders in a way that the market doesn't currently provide.

Ours is a leadership experience that is **values-based**. It is a leadership ethos that deals with **relationships at the core** and transactions as secondary.

We exist to develop integral leaders of tomorrow.

CHAPTER 28

PERSONAL DEVELOPMENT

n reality, every person is coming to us for personal development. Their presenting issue may be their career or a relational conflict or a self-defeating personal habit, but they want us to help them be a better and more fulfilled spouse, parent, friend, leader, and coworker. Those who want help in personal development often make more progress more quickly because they're already eager to learn and grow.

Great leadership does not mean running away from reality. Sometimes the hard truths might just demoralize the company, but at other times sharing difficulties can inspire people to take action that will make the situation better.

—JOHN KOTTER

The primary goal of someone we coach may be a raised level of confidence, better communication skills, replacing a bad habit with a constructive one, or honing a skill to be more effective.

FIVE AREAS

Many coaching models identify five areas of personal development, so we can target our efforts to address one, some, or all of them with a particular person. These are:

1) **Physical**
   - We can discuss the need for improvement in exercise and create a reasonable and effective regimen to get in better shape. An elliptical machine may help, but walking has proven to be one of the very best exercises.
   - We can discuss healthy eating habits, which is difficult but not impossible for busy people. Many different experts offer clear and comprehensive diet plans, and many of them tailor their recommendations for people with particular health concerns.
   - And we can discuss sleep patterns. The Center for Disease Control recommends teenagers get 8 to 10 hours of sleep each day, and adults 18 to 60 years old should get at least seven hours a day. Those older than sixty require 7 to 9 hours. Sleep disorders are an epidemic today, so coaches should spend time carefully analyzing a person's sleep patterns and recommend resources for better sleep.

2) **Mental**

■ As we saw in Part 2, "Building Hope," one of our most important contributions to a person's well-being is "bringing past hopes and successes into the present and exchanging ANTS into PETS." ANTS are Automatic Negative Thoughts, and PETS are Performance-Enhancing Thoughts. Many people live in a secret, dark world of poisonous thinking. They focus on what they've done wrong, who is upset with them, and how nothing ever works out for them. These ANTS are deeply embedded in their thinking, and they don't just vanish. They must be replaced, gradually and intentionally, by PETS.

■ It's wise for coaches to help people craft a few positive, life-affirming statements, write them on a card, memorize them, and repeat them until they have the ascendency in the person's mind and heart. We can also recommend books, audios, podcasts, and music that communicate a positive message that the one we're coaching can internalize.

3) **Emotional**

■ The ANTS aren't just thoughts; they feed painful emotions of hurt, fear, anger, and shame. As the ANTS are identified and replaced, those we coach often feel a great sense of relief and begin to feel love, kindness, respect, gratitude, and joy. Again, this is usually a gradual process, one that people intuitively fight against because it feels so new—and even wrong. Emotional healing includes the difficult process of grieving losses, and no one grieves well alone.

4) **Social**

- We are social animals. We may be introverts, but even introverts need a few close friends. And extroverts often have friendships that are a bit superficial. Introverts need to develop close relationships with a few, so they need the courage to reach out. And extroverts need to find a few honest, loving people among their throng of connections, so they need the courage to go deeper.

- Those who come to us for help may have been deeply hurt in the past—as children, in an unhappy marriage, with wayward children, at work, or by former friends. Grieving, forgiving, and healing are necessary components to clear the way forward to healthier, more authentic relationships.

5) **Spiritual**

- We're not only social; we're also spiritual. We may have very different ways of connecting with the supernatural, but the vast majority of us are convinced there's a world—and a Being— beyond our five senses. Coaches can explore spiritual desires and expectations, and make recommendations of books, prayer journals, and other resources to stimulate this part of a person's life.

To acknowledge you were wrong yesterday
is to acknowledge you are wiser today.
—CHARLES H. SPURGEON

THREE STAGES

Experts in the area of personal development identify three distinct stages of progress:

1) Raising Self-awareness

The coach's role is to ask good questions to clarify goals, identify hindrances, and explore the payoffs of progress.

2) Crafting a New Identity

Steps forward give others a refreshing sense of who they are, what they can do, and where they're going. They may have seen themselves as barely competent before, and they've tried to hide their self-doubts in any of a myriad of ways, but now they begin to genuinely believe in themselves.

3) Developing New Skills

We often think of skills related to work, but we also can develop skills related to the five areas of personal growth. Each area is a canvas on which people can paint a new, better version of themselves.

In a *Forbes* article encouraging leaders to dedicate themselves to personal development, Andrew Rains recommends four important components:

1) **Put it in writing.** Create a written plan to hold yourself accountable and put time on your calendar to chip away at growth mindset goals. Take the same discipline you apply to other areas in your life—like never missing a daily workout—and apply that dedication to your personal growth.

2) **Find a time commitment that works for you.** People often ask me how I have time to dedicate to personal growth. For me, it's because I listen to books on Audible. Don't set yourself up for failure by setting unrealistic goals. Maybe reading one book per month isn't realistic for you. What about ten minutes a day? Or two audiobooks per month? Set yourself up for success by committing to an obtainable goal.

3) **Collaborate to create accountability.** Hopefully, you won't go through this journey alone, and you can find others in your company to forge a bond with and help hold each other accountable. One idea that's worked well for my company is a professional development book club. It's been great to see how several other book clubs have spawned from the original one.

4) **Stay curious.** Curiosity goes hand in hand with a personal growth mindset. When you stay curious, you don't fall into a fixed mindset. Make why and how frequent parts of your vocabulary, and commit to an "always be learning" mindset—even if you've reached the pinnacle of your career.[73]

These can become elements we communicate to others, so they can use them to continue growing.

Coaching people toward personal development is often rewarding for the coach and life-changing for the person. They've come to us because they have at least a glimmer of a new vision for their future, and we have the honor of stepping in to help them think more clearly, craft their goals, and take bold steps to a better life.

---

73 "How to Develop a Personal Growth Mindset that Fuels Business Success," Andrew Rains, Forbes, December 21, 2020, https://www.forbes.com/sites/forbesbusinessdevelopmentcouncil/2020/12/21/how-to-develop-a-personal-growth-mindset-that-fuels-business-success/?sh=793afc4725b0.

Avoiding the phrase "I don't have time...," will soon help you to realize that you do have the time needed for just about anything you choose to accomplish in life.

—BO BENNETT, AUTHOR OF *YEAR TO SUCCESS*

NEVER STOP GROWING

MIKE KAI

Senior Pastor, Inspire Church & Founder of Inspire Collective; Master Coach Trainer, Dream Releaser Coaching

At some point in an executive's career, it's inevitable to sense a plateau or a roadblock looming on the horizon. While some may view this as impending doom, can I let you in on a little secret? This is actually a gift! Because the mere fact that we can see it approaching gives us the opportunity to prepare for it.

If you are aware, you can do whatever it takes to avoid or take advantage of what's coming. Essentially, your foresight can help you navigate yourself and your company through these difficult waters.

That's why it's so important to find a coach. I've hired an executive coach on several occasions. If you've ever been to a gym, you understand how much better your results can be when you have a partner. When you hire a trainer, you learn the best techniques, find the right motivation, and have someone to help you achieve your goals.

Nobody climbs Mount Everest without a Sherpa. Since Sir Edmund Hillary and Tenzing Norgay were the first to reach the summit of the world's highest mountain in 1953, it's been apparent that success—in climbing mountains or corporate ladders—is contingent on strategic alliances. Climbers need Sherpas, athletes need trainers, and top executives need hired coaches.

When I engage a client, it's under the assumption that it'll be one-on-one. I'll ask a lot of questions to understand how I can add value to the particular area of life (business, health and nutrition, etc.) that will also enhance personal development (confidence, self-awareness, etc.). It largely involves changing their perspective from half empty to half full, negative to positive, scarcity to abundance, self-defeating to God-declaring.

Coaching is individual, but consulting is corporate. Consulting borrows from aspects of coaching, like asking powerful questions and mining for the "gold" in people, but consulting looks at the culture of the team, the systems and structures, communication (both verbal and nonverbal), and assists the corporate executives in sharpening their vision and accomplishing their goals.

Coaching is a wise investment. If you've watched *The Last Dance*, the documentary series about the Chicago Bulls' epic run at six NBA championships (and I have at least eleven times), in several episodes you would've seen interviews with Michael Jordan's personal trainer, Tim Grover. Phil Jackson was Jordan's coach on the basketball court, but Grover was his coach in the weight room. Six rings, ten scoring titles, five MVP Awards, ten All-NBA First Team designations, nine All-Defensive First Team honors, fourteen NBA All-Star Game selections, and three All-Star Game MVP Awards tell the tale because hardware doesn't lie. A good coach helps clients objectively see their unique circumstances and provides them with the tools they need to deal with the specifics of their situations. The right coach helps them accelerate learning, improve critical thinking skills, increase self-awareness, and improve their interactions with a team (because almost all of us work with teams). An effective coach helps them discover their blind spots, recognize destructive thinking patterns, and flip the script on self-talk, so they can break barriers and set records.

Post-pandemic, there are more methods than ever for coaching. From scheduled Zoom calls and phone calls to webinars, clients no longer have to be in physical proximity to benefit from coaching.

While some people may think they don't need a coach, especially if they're self-starters, I'm discovering that more people are actually looking for that extra nudge a coach provides. If executives want to go further, they need to change the trajectory of their focus and consider who's walking alongside them.

CHAPTER 29

WEIGHT CONTROL

By the time people come to us to ask for help with a weight problem, they've usually tried multiple diet plans, bought exercise equipment that's now gathering dust in the garage, and beaten themselves up innumerable times for being such a failure. Our role, then, is to restore hope, instill a new vision for weight control, and provide some clear tracks for them to run on.

THE MAGNITUDE OF THE PROBLEM

The Center for Disease Control found that 42.4% of American adults qualify as obese, and in recent years, severe obesity increased from 4.7% to 9.2%. The problem isn't just that people feel uncomfortable or feel ashamed; there are very real health risks. Obesity is a contributing factor in heart disease, stroke, type 2 diabetes, certain types of cancer, deterioration of joints, and other diseases and conditions. It is one of the leading causes of premature death. The most recent estimate is that medical costs for obesity approach $150 billion annually, or about $1,500 more than for people whose weight is in the normal range.[74]

Diets alone may be the answer for some, but many people gain much of the weight back, and some even more, after their diet ends. An article in *Scientific American* states:

> *Research suggests that roughly 80% of people who shed a signif-icant portion of their body fat will not maintain that degree of weight loss for 12 months; and, according to one meta-analysis of intervention studies, dieters regain, on average, more than half of what they lose within two years. Meanwhile, follow-up care that is meant to stave off this backsliding via behavioral or life-style interventions appears to be effective only at the margins: across several dozen randomized trials, the benefits of these programs—in terms of minimizing regain—were pretty small at two years, and undetectable thereafter. In short, we've known for quite some time that while it's hard to lose weight, it's even harder to keep it off.[75]*

CAUSES

Physicians, nutritionists, and psychologists have identified a number of factors that can lead to problems with weight control.

1) Slow Metabolism

Everyone would like to think there's a medical cause of their weight problem, and for some, it is, in fact, the real source. Their bodies don't

74 "Adult Obesity Facts," CDC, https://www.cdc.gov/obesity/data/adult.html.
75 "Unexpected Clues Emerge about Why Diets Fail," Daniel Engber, Scientific American, January 13, 2020, https://www.scientificamerican.com/article/unexpected-clues-emerge-about-why-diets-fail/.

process calories quickly enough. An article by the Harvard Medical School states: "Metabolism or metabolic rate is defined as *the series of chemical reactions in a living organism that create and break down energy necessary for life*. More simply, it's the rate at which your body expends energy or burns calories. . . . Metabolism is partly genetic and largely outside of one's control. Changing it is a matter of considerable debate. Some people are just lucky. They inherited genes that promote a faster metabolism and can eat more than others without gaining weight. Others are not so lucky and end up with a slow metabolism."[76]

2) Poor Impulse Control

This is a far more prevalent cause of weight gain. It's easy to eat an extra helping, another cookie, a snack between meals, and supersize the order . . . just this once.

3) Lack of Exercise

This problem becomes self-reinforcing because people who are overweight don't feel like exercising, which leads to them feeling more sluggish, making exercise even less appealing.

4) Emotional Eating

Past abuse, abandonment, and other emotional deficits—as well as current emotional distress—can cause some people to see food as their chief source of comfort, but others see food as a threat. Three major categories of emotional eating are anorexia (avoiding food to the point of life-threatening malnutrition), bulimia (cycles of bingeing and purging), and compulsive overeating.

76 "Does Metabolism Matter in Weight Loss?" Harvard Health Publishing, July 2015, https://www.health.harvard.edu/diet-and-weight-loss/does-metabolism-matter-in-weight-loss.

5) Bad Habits

Over their lifetimes, many people have developed routines, almost rituals, regarding food. They have a box of chocolates on their desk, they put an extra piece of bread in the toaster, they go to the refrigerator several times a day to grab a bite, or some other behavior that gets them a quick hit of satisfaction but add hundreds of calories to their daily intake. Quite often, these habits are so ingrained that they seem completely normal.

And of course, it's certainly possible for several of these causes to contribute to the problem.

RESISTANCE AND PAYOFFS

As we coach people who want a healthier lifestyle, we can expect plenty of resistance. They may complain that change is too hard, or they may insist that nothing will work for them. More often, people have initial enthusiasm followed by growing complaints when they realize they really do need to change their lifestyle, and it isn't going to be easy or fast.

At the beginning and throughout the coaching relationship, focus on the payoffs. What will the person gain by making the decisions to live better? Some want to look good in a bathing suit on a cruise they're planning for six months later, others may want to get in shape to run in a race or play a sport without carrying so much extra baggage, others just want to feel better so they can be more energetic with their children or grandchildren, and some want to be sharper and more agile at work. Beneath these goals, many people want to escape the shame of hating themselves when they look in the mirror. They need us to give them hope that the difficult changes they're making are well worth the effort and sacrifice.

PRACTICAL STEPS

There are, as you know, countless books, podcasts, programs, and organizations that make promises and offer assistance to those who are motivated to control their weight. These often include:

See a Doctor

People need to determine if there are any underlying conditions that need to be addressed and ask for advice about how to proceed. Some may want to consider gastric sleeve surgery, but even then, they'll need to make some changes in nutrition and exercise. But others may have the opposite problem: Anorexia is a serious medical condition and requires the intervention of a physician. Bulimia isn't usually life-threatening, but it's a compulsive behavior that has a powerful and detrimental impact on every part of the person's life.

Set a Goal

It needs to be a "Goldilocks goal"—not so big that it's unattainable but not so small that it doesn't motivate. The goal should be categorized in short-term, mid-term, and long-term segments. For instance, the short-term goal might be to lose two pounds a week for ten weeks, the mid-term goal would be to look and feel better at a wedding that's scheduled months away, and a long-term goal might be remain at a certain weight for the rest of their lives.

Develop a Plan

The plan needs to address every element of a healthy lifestyle, and it should be as detailed as possible. For instance, some people go to the grocery store without a list, and impulse buying is the inescapable result.

So, making a list is part of the plan. Other elements are an exercise regimen, sleep schedule, serving portions, snacks, etc.

Value Slow and Steady Progress

One of the main reasons people quit a weight-control plan is that they don't see dramatic results in a short period of time. That's unrealistic, and in fact, counterproductive. Those we coach may have aggressive long-term goals, like losing one hundred pounds, but they need very realistic short- and mid-term goals.

Identify the Speedbumps

Help your friend or client identify the most likely ways they can slip up. They may need to put a sign on the refrigerator door to keep it closed except when they're preparing meals, they may need to avoid having cookies or sweets in the house, or they may need to set an alarm to get up earlier to get out of bed to exercise. All of us have weak spots. The person you're helping needs to do some preventative maintenance to avoid giving in to them.

Celebrate Small Wins

Every step forward is remarkable, and celebrating them is important to keep the level of motivation high . . . but not with a big slice of cake!

Change a Lifestyle—Don't Just Go on a Diet

As we've seen, people who are focused only on caloric intake quite often reach their desired weight goal but soon gain much (or all or more) of it back. Our role as coaches is to change the narrative—the person isn't just going on a diet; he or she is now committed to a healthy lifestyle that has payoffs in every aspect of life and all relationships.

Give Supportive Accountability

Many people already know what they need to do, but they've failed in the past because they didn't have anyone to be a cheerleader or hold them to their commitments. They need us to continually inject hope and inspire courage as they face temptations to quit the process, and they need us to ask kind but honest questions. They may say they don't like these questions, but actually, that's why they hired us.

Provide Reminders

You might recommend putting a note on the refrigerator or their bathroom mirror to remind them to be strong. These PETs (Performance-Enhancing Thoughts) are both poignant and witty:

- "When you eat crap, you feel like crap."
- "Don't dig your grave with a knife and fork."
- "When you feel like quitting, think about why you started."
- "Every step is progress, no matter how small."
- "One pound at a time."
- "A year from now, you'll wish you had started today."
- "The past can't be changed. The future is in your hands today."
- "There's no such thing as failure. Either you win or you learn."

CHAPTER 30

TRANSCULTURAL COACHING

O ver the years, my husband, Sam, has taken our family back several times to his hometown in India. From the moment we get off the plane, I realize I've stepped into another world. Sam transitions easily from one culture to another . . . because he has lived so long in both worlds, but in India, I have a choice: to retreat (mentally, emotionally, and maybe physically), so I won't feel uncomfortable in the unfamiliar culture, or jump in with both feet, engaging even when I don't quite know what's going on and asking questions to learn as much as I can.

It's easy to notice the differences in cultures when we travel overseas, but there are significant differences in our own country. People of different races, ethnicity, languages, socio-economic backgrounds, and political persuasions may live next door! For a variety of reasons, it seems that people today are more polarized, angrier, and more suspicious of "the others," whoever they may be. Many feel completely comfortable—and even more, *right*—in their contempt for those who don't look like them, don't talk like them, don't believe like them, and don't vote like them. If we want to build bridges across the divides, we need to enter into the world of others, seeking to understand far more than to be understood, listening far more than talking, and not stopping until we can articulate the values and passions of the other person as well (or better) than they can. That's a tall order, but it's exactly the right prescription for coaches who want to help people who aren't like them. It's a challenging but rewarding opportunity.

WHAT IS CULTURE?

An Australian article about transcultural connections explains:

Cultures have visible and hidden elements. Visible cultural features include artifacts, symbols, and practices; art and architecture; language, colour, and dress; and social etiquette and traditions.

But visible cultural differences are only ten percent of our cultural identities; hidden cultural differences including values, assumptions, and beliefs represent the remaining ninety percent of our cultural identity.

Values are the central feature of a culture. They shape tangible cultural differences. For example, a cultural emphasis on success is reflected in achievement-orientated characteristics like competitive economic systems—for example, capitalism, child-rearing practices that encourage and reward achievement, a high prevalence of status symbols such as luxury goods, heroes

*who have accumulated great wealth or fame, and the acceptance
and promotion of assertive and ambitious behaviour.*[77]

Every country, region, race, gender, and organization creates a distinct culture. Over years, generations, and perhaps centuries, they have
constructed and reinforced a way of seeing, a way of believing, and a
way of acting. In each one, the culture is "how things are done here."

Of course, some values are constant across cultures. For instance,
most religions have some version of the "Golden Rule," and family relationships form the bedrock of every society. But beneath these obvious
elements, people can be very, very different. If coaches aren't aware of a
person's unique perspectives and assumptions, they'll almost certainly
be less than effective.

Some of the most common differences are:

- Some cultures use shame and honor to motivate people and
  control behavior. The threat of ridicule or ostracism from the
  safety of the group is powerful, and those who break the rules
  may become victims of revenge from those who keep them. On
  the other hand, other cultures appeal to morality and use guilt
  and fear, as well as the threat of punishment now or in eternity.
  These cultures also may use physical or political power to force
  compliance. Authoritarian countries are examples of this kind
  of culture.

- So, when you're coaching someone from a shame and honor
  culture, even mild criticism is often a crushing blow, so you don't
  talk to that person like you would to someone who is used to
  people demanding compliance.

77 "Nine Cultural Value Differences You Need to Know," Include-Empower.com, https://
cultureplusconsulting.com/2015/06/23/nine-cultural-value-differences-you-need-to-know/.

- In northern European countries, people are considered late if they arrive more than ten minutes after the appointment was scheduled, but in many other countries, it's perfectly acceptable (and normal) to be at least thirty minutes late to any meeting—and on the island of Yap in the Pacific, you can be four hours late without anyone getting upset!

- So, when you coach someone from a culture that has a loose concept of time, you'll need to make sure you allot more time for your meeting because it won't get started on time. And if you press the person to be on time, he'll be offended by your insistence.

- Some cultures are egalitarian and have high regard for the role of women, but others are male-dominated.

- So, when you coach a woman from a culture where women seldom rise to any level of leadership, don't be surprised by the reluctance and even a feeling of shame for even considering a promotion.

- Similarly, some cultures accept power differentials without question. Everyone knows their place, and no one is expected to rise above their status. Other cultures are much more fluid, and it's widely applauded when people have "from rags to riches" stories.

- So, when you coach someone who doesn't have much hope for progress, you'll need to go the extra mile in helping the person have a fresh, bold vision . . . and act on it.

- Some cultures are very assertive, and people are quite blunt in their communication, but others are far more cautious and consider the feelings of the other person.

- So, if you're coaching someone from an assertive culture, don't be surprised by brusque comments, demands, and criticism. It may feel like an assault to you, but it's entirely normal for them.

- Some cultures, especially those with rigid, fundamentalist religions, speak with certainty, and see delays and questions as weakness. Other cultures value ambiguity and feel comfortable taking the time to explore different views and ideas.

- So, if you're coaching someone from a strict religious background, the person may not feel comfortable with a lengthy process of exploration. You may need to pick up the pace and be sensitive to the need for certainty.

- Some cultures are individualistic, and people think of their own goals, their own pleasure, and their own power over others. Other cultures are collective, and groups (primarily families) are more important than the individuals.

- So, when you coach someone from a collective culture, you'll need to show how the person's vision and progress positively affect the rest of the family, the team, and others in the sphere of relationships.

EFFECTIVE TRANSCULTURAL COACHING

As smart and gifted people from other cultures enter our world, we have more opportunities to coach transculturally. To be effective, we need to follow this path:

Understand Yourself

You and your culture are just as different from others as they seem different from you. The first step, then, is to take a long, hard look at how your culture has shaped your values, expectations, prejudices, and behavior. And yes, we all have prejudices, likes and dislikes, things that make us comfortable and those that feel awkward . . . and wrong. This isn't an easy reflection because we're so immersed in our own culture that everything about it feels completely good, right, and normal. For that reason, we seldom if ever spend time analyzing the impact our culture has on us. If we don't grasp the unique pressures and contributions of our own culture, we can't be sensitive to others.

Value Differences

Don't just notice the differences—racists do that! But go much further to learn to appreciate the food, dress, faith, stories, and pleasures of other cultures. This can be as simple as asking a person for a recommendation of an ethnic restaurant (and perhaps meeting your friend or client there), to exploring the elements (listed and described under "What Is Culture?") and the impact of the person's culture.

Explore New and Effective Strategies

All of us have our "bent," our go-to coaching strategies that work for those who are at least somewhat like us, but those strategies may not connect with the mind and heart of those from another culture. Take time to ask questions about how successful people in that culture operate, what gives them direction and drive, and what barriers they have to overcome. Previous assumptions about "the way things work" need to be ground up and reformed—if not thrown out and replaced, at least for that person.

Connect with Empathy

You can take it for granted that people from other cultures—either from the other side of town, another part of the country, or from across the globe—feel unsettled. The marches and riots about racial injustice aren't just clips in the news for some people we coach—it's at the heart of who they are and who they want to become. And people from other lands already feel insecure about their language skills and many other aspects of our culture that aren't familiar and comfortable. Take plenty of time to get to know them, to show that they're more than a slot in your schedule, and to fully enter their hopes, fears, and dreams.

Practice Immediacy

As we make fewer assumptions, we'll find moments when we need to say, "Wait a second. Tell me more about that. I want to understand." This tells them that we're fully engaged, we value them so much that we want to slow down to grasp what they're really saying, and we're a safe place in their unfamiliar and often threatening world.

Transcultural coaching is no longer just a concept; it's the wave of the future as globalization makes it much easier to connect with people who may have been "the others" before, but they can become genuine friends.

PART 5

Coaching as a Business

CHAPTER 31

CHOOSING YOUR NICHE

Generalist or specialist? This is an important question for people in numerous professions and careers. Typically, education, experience, success, and reputation—or a combination of all these factors—will set an individual apart. We have found this to be true in the field of professional coaching. Obviously, there are generalists who do quite well across the spectrum of professions; however, clients like to feel they are understood and served by someone whose talents and experience uniquely fit their needs.

A coaching niche is a specialization in a particular area—a type of industry or service company, a type of client, or particular leadership skills—and having expertise in that area. Identifying your niche helps you focus on potential clients as you market your coaching practice. Instead of being a generic life coach in a saturated market, you can set yourself apart and stand out as a specialty coach.

When considering your niche, focus on two primary factors: your experience and the needs of potential clients. This will define your optimum opportunity to have an impact on others. This has been called "coaching to the gap."[78]

Most coaches who specialize believe their reputations spread more rapidly when they branded themselves as coaches with targeted, specific expertise. In a survey on niche coaching, three advantages surfaced. They are:

1) You know how to target your marketing.

2) You know who your clients are.

3) You know specifically what your clients are looking for.

Finding your niche provides a profitable and fulfilling focus for your coaching practice, while at the same time, you work with people who need and value what you offer. Identifying your niche enables you to attract a steady stream of ideal clients who value your particular expertise and contribution into their lives.

Clients are looking for specific outcomes, not broad and random input. When prospective clients learn that you offer a service that is custom-designed for them, they are much more likely to sign up and enroll in the process. As a coach, you want to stand out as someone who is speaking directly to the heart of what a person wants and needs. According to Ryan Magdziarz, author of *Secrets of the 7 Figure Coach*, in order to have a profitable niche, you need three things:

1) **A Problem**—the most painful area in someone's life right now.

2) **A Promise**—the best possible solution for the problem.

---

78 Gary Collins, Christian Coaching: Helping Others Turn Potential into Reality, 304.

3) **Proficiency**—your ability to deliver the results you have promised.

There are many benefits of a clearly defined coaching niche, including:

- **Lower Start-Up Costs**—Knowing your niche means there are no wasted business cards, no expense in revising your website, and no unnecessary marketing changes that result in extra costs.
- **Less Competition**—The narrower your niche, the fewer coaches who are offering the same services.
- **Reputation Building**—Word of mouth is a powerful marketing tool. Clients who are thrilled with specific, targeted coaching input will tell their friends and associates.
- **Specific Differentiation**—Tailoring your business to meet specific needs assures your clients you will stay focused on what matters to them.
- **Boosting Your Authority**—Showing your expertise in a specific field establishes you as a thought leader. You will be known as a valued expert.

THE RIGHT NICHE FOR YOU

Your niche should be the confluence of your interests, skills, and experience, as well as the recurring needs of your clients. The following questions may require research into your field of interest, attending various workshops to sharpen your skills, and time to interview prospective clients. Consider each of the following areas:

- Passion: What is an area that excites you? What needs or desires of your clients cause your enthusiasm to increase?

- A Burning Need: What problems would you like to help your clients solve? How does your expertise or knowledge in this area contribute to your clients' success?

- Identify an Underserved Audience: Is your arena of choice saturated with competitors? Where can you find more information about the needs for your services or expertise?

- Precedent: Have others targeted the market with this niche before? Have coaches in this niche found success financially in your local area?

- Be First: Does your research support your being a "trailblazer" as the first in a specialized area, such as being the first coach for hearing-impaired high school students preparing for the SAT or ACT?

- Discretionary Income: Can prospective clients pay for your services? Can they earmark your coaching fees as an educational or business expense?

- Narrow Focus: Can you justify limiting your scope to a selected market and still be profitable?

- Specialized Group: Have you identified professional or specialized organizations that have state or national affiliations?

- Method of Marketing: How will you communicate with prospects? What is the most cost-effective method of reaching your potential clients?

- Time and Money: Is your niche meeting only a short-term need, or does it involve a continual service for which clients are willing to pay over a longer time frame?

- Partnership Niche: Can you develop a partnership with another coach who shares the same interest or who is already successful?

POPULAR NICHES

A number of websites and books address the topic of coaching niches. We gleaned the following list from the internet by using the keywords "niche coaching" and "niche marketing."

The following niche ideas can stand alone or be combined to enhance your coaching business:

Arts and Creativity

Acting, dancing, music, singing, writing, drawing, painting, crafts, photography

Career

Advancement, career transition, interview skills, job search, retirement, success

Corporate

Executive coaching, mergers and acquisitions, strategic planning, team building, conflict resolution

Family

Adoption, aging parents, planning a funeral, living overseas, military family, mixed families, parenting, single parenting, stay-at-home parent

Health, Fitness, Wellness

Competitive sports, exercise, nutrition, specific diets, specific health problems, weight loss

Life Skills

Assertiveness, communication skills (effective listening, questioning, rapport building, etc.), self-confidence, time management, work/life balance, financial management, getting organized (declutter), interior design, lifestyle design, personal image

Love/Relationships

Cross-cultural, dealing with loss, divorce, marriage

Performance

Goal setting and achievement, motivation, productivity, wealth

Professional Skills

Communication, customer service, leadership, management, negotiations, project management, public relations, public speaking, sales/marketing

Small Business

Entrepreneur, starting a business, growing a business, using the internet for marketing and sales

Spirituality

Inner peace, intuition, life purpose, meditation, mid-life crisis, religion

Shared Common Ground

Specific age, location, nationality, profession, religion, life experiences

You may want to consult the following websites for more information on coaching niches:

- 101 Real Coaching Niches
- 99 Coaching Niches
- The Christian Coaching Center

DEVELOPING YOUR COACHING NICHE

TERESITA GLASGOW

Author, Speaker, Coach; President/CEO: In His Season, Inc.
Consulting; Founder: Destiny Dreamer Coaching

One of the most important things that you will need to do as a coach is to identify who your clients are and their needs. Who are the people who need your services? This is as important for your clients as it is for you. You have already gotten your coaching certifications; you have invested hours of study to know your skillset. You have invested time and money, but now you need to determine where exactly your skills will benefit you and your clients. There are several areas in which most people seek to be coached: Time, Money/Finance, Health, Love/Romance, and Spirituality. In the book, *Book Yourself Solid*, the acronym FEPS is used to identify four areas: Financial, Emotional, Physical and Spiritual—this is helpful when you are trying to identify your niche.

Merriam Webster defines a niche as "a place, employment, status, or activity for which a person or thing is best fitted." You have a specific gift, and now you have been trained as a coach. Somewhere between your natural gift and your level of training and life experiences is your niche. Discovering our niche is often a process of discovery. In other words, you may already be coaching using the basics before you discover an area where you realize that you have a special insight and understanding. This area repeatedly allows you to help your clients move from where they are to where they want to be.

By using the basic coaching tools such as questionnaires, exercises, and homework assignments, you and your client begin to uncover hidden dreams and interests. This insight also will determine the area in which the client really needs to be coached. I call this the "drill down" because I have discovered that the real issue is often below the surface. For example, your client may be having a problem with a supervisor, but as you move forward with several coaching sessions, you discover that your client has had problems with his last five supervisors. That is an indication that a deeper dive or drill down is needed, and a different line of questioning is in order. You need to ask questions that lead your client toward introspection because the same difficulties are recurring. The problem may be the supervisors, but because the variable in the situation is the supervisors and the client is the only constant, something else may be going on. This is an opportunity to explore a pattern and find a solution.

My life experiences have given me a broad knowledge base. I attended a vocational high school and was licensed as a cosmetologist, and I worked in the beauty industry as a hairdresser off and on for over a decade. I attended college as an adult while I was also raising my two children as a single parent. After college I entered an entirely different career. I joined corporate America and worked within the corporate trust industry, a financial service business with the capital markets. I worked on Wall Street in New York City and Atlanta, Georgia, for nearly two decades. During my time in the industry, I moved from entry level to Vice President and Relationship Manager. Throughout those years, I also continued my education and received certification as a Certified Corporate Trust Specialist. I have also spent time in the government contract sector. Each one of these industries works differently and has its own culture. This breadth of experience gives me leverage when it comes to listening and discerning a client's career and personal development needs. Many career decisions require a deep dive because the struggle is internal. The mixture of your life experiences and your coach training are assets to be used during your coaching sessions.

If you are a Christian Life Coach, your relationship to and knowledge of Scripture are important. Not all your clients will be Christians, but all people are spiritual on some level, even if they are not aware of it. Having a certain amount of sensitivity to your clients' understanding of themselves is important. Of course, if your client is a Christian, you may also connect in your sessions on a spiritual level using Scripture.

I discovered my niche at the intersection of business, career, and spirituality. My clients are usually in transition in career or in life. A lot of introspection and a willingness to self-confront is necessary, so I often use the GROW model (G=Goals, R=Reality, O=Options, W=Will). The GROW model takes the client through the steps to identify their goals, confront the reality of where they currently are, and identify the barriers. The client's motivation is paramount. Coaching only works if the client is eager to do the work necessary to reach the goal.

My niche is Transformational Coaching, which is a broad statement. Transformation can come in many areas, including career, aging, divorce, occupation, and spiritual growth. The list can go on and on. The principles of personal growth and development are transferrable to every area of the client's life.

One of my clients was working in the medical field but wanted to move to the legal side of the profession. She did not realize what she really wanted until she received some life coaching for several work-related issues. As we worked together, she gained enough confidence to begin to dream very different dreams. We accomplished a good deal of deep introspection, and she reconnected with her desire to move into the legal side of the medical profession. She was able to get into a college program and complete the required course of study. She is now working in her dream profession.

Developing a broad clientele in your niche is an acquired skill. In addition to your coaching expertise, the optimal term to remember is "systems" because your coaching business will need to be branded and marketed. The following questions will need to be answered: "Who are you? And why should I choose you as my coach?" You must answer these questions in your marketing materials and get the word out using systems, including word of mouth, website, publications, social media, online classes, etc. These systems will assist you to get the visibility that you need to attract more coaching clients. A good tagline will enhance the marketing of your coaching business.

A tagline is a statement that will introduce who you are, what you do, and what is in it for them. For example, my tagline is: "I coach professional women to soar past their fears, free up their time, rediscover their dreams, and reignite their passion to live the life they've always dreamed of!" Coaching is extremely competitive, so it is important to know your own uniqueness.

Happy coaching!

DEVELOPING YOUR COACHING NICHE

KAREN ROBERTSON

Co-Lead Pastor, Visalia First Assembly of God; Master Coach Trainer, Dream Releaser Coaching

According to the Urban Dictionary (Peckham, 1999) the term "niche" in today's English has come to mean:

1) A position or activity that particularly suits somebody's talents and personality or that somebody can make his or her own.
2) An area of the market specializing in one type of product or service.
3) Place in nature: The role of an organism within its natural environment that determines its relations with other organisms and ensures its survival.
4) A recess in a wall, especially one made to hold a statue.
5) Hollow place: any recess or hollow, e.g. in a rock formation.

For our purposes, we will stick to definitions one, two, and three. We will leave definitions four and five to the philosophers and preachers, so they can tell us imaginative ways to apply them metaphorically. Actually, I relate most to number three: "Place in nature: The role of an organism within its natural environment that determines its relations with other organisms and *ensures* its survival."

By looking at all five meanings, we can see that a niche is our natural habitat, something that houses our passion, that makes us want to get out of bed in the morning. It can be *where* you work or *how* you work, *how* to connect with people, your talents, skills, or what you are most productive in.

HOW I DISCOVERED MY NICHE

I used to feel I had a talent for staying busy. My mother was always busy, and my father was always busy. They were my models. In my very first job at sixteen, when I worked at a pharmacy making deliveries and filing paperwork, my mother gave me this advice: "Always find something to do. When you run out of something to do, grab a bottle of Windex and clean the counter, cabinet handles, and anything else within arm's reach." And I loved being busy.

But I also loved music. To my siblings' surprise—because practicing the piano was a chore for them—no one ever had to tell me to practice. As a child and teenager, I also had a strong affinity toward God and the things of God. I combined these elements in my major of Music Education and minor of Christian Education, and that's where I met the man who was to be my husband.

For years, I partnered with my husband in pastoring while using my passion for music to develop musical teams and productions, but I became all things to all people. That satisfied my need for busyness and fulfilled the belief that staying busy was of utmost importance. However, it left a dissatisfaction in the depths of my soul that I was *good* at many things, but no longer *great* at my soul's desire.

Once I began to focus strongly on using my passion for music as a vehicle to minister to people, it satisfied the two strongest passions in my life. And because it *is a passion*, it definitely keeps me busy, gets me up in the morning, causes me to open my calendar and my planning journal, and propels me toward the future.

What does this have to do with developing a niche in coaching? As I entered a new season in life, I had a strong desire to help others get unstuck, so they could move toward their passions and into their areas of skill, giftings, productivity, and promotion. I have years of experience in working on these areas in my life—focusing on my skill development, giftings and productivity—and it has led to fulfillment in the two areas I am passionate about. I can help others because I am building relational capital. Partly because I know how it feels to be where they are, I have empathy and can help them take steps forward.

My focus on church worship, music, building and leading teams, stage dynamics, seasonal productions, time management, ministry and promotion all come from a comfortable and seasoned place in me. The ease with which I can approach each client in these pursuits is because this niche is internalized in me, and it gives me joy to see others succeed. That's how I found my niche in coaching.

HOW WILL YOU DISCOVER YOUR NICHE?

1) Make a list of areas you are passionate about.
2) Write a list of compliments others have given you when you are doing something you enjoy.
3) Compare these lists and see which passionate areas have the most positive feedback to you from others.
4) Now rank your list of areas you were passionate about.
5) Narrow that ranking down to the top three.
6) Look at those top three and ask yourself:
   - If I could only do one of these, which one could I not live without?
   - Which one of these am I most gifted in and skilled at?
   - Which one of these meets a need that is common enough to have consistent income that will support me either part-time or full-time?
7) Name Your Niche.

HOW DO YOU DEVELOP A COACHING CLIENTELE IN YOUR NICHE?

1) Word of mouth: There are people in your life that observe what you do well. They can be your greatest advocates.

2) Research coaching companies looking for partners within your niche.

3) Develop a marketing plan for social media. There are online courses to teach best practices.

4) Referrals. Leave your information at :

- Offices of counselors. Many times, a person is not in need of counseling but coaching. The counselor can refer those people to you. In return, you can also tell the counselor's office that you will refer clients to them when you know people are in need of counseling instead of coaching.

- Hairdressers. People share their stories there.

- Join coaching circles and network.

5) Offer a finder's discount to clients who refer someone who books an appointment.

CHAPTER 32

ORGANIZING YOUR BUSINESS

W hy do so many businesses fail? What can you do to assure a higher probability of success in your coaching business? We have found that many gifted coaches don't understand what's involved in organizing and operating the business of coaching.

COST/BENEFIT ANALYSIS

Starting a business involves planning, making key financial decisions, and filing a series of legal papers. It isn't for the faint of heart. It's stressful and demands your complete focus. Paradoxically, the best path of growth is to create the chaos of change early enough to take advantage of existing momentum. In this way, we move into new areas of challenge in order to achieve greater growth.

Starting a business often involves stepping out of one's comfort zone, away from what has been a place of security. As a coach, we are taught to empower our clients to DOL (dream out loud) and not allow their past to dictate their future. We ask powerful questions that will dislodge them from being stuck, so they can find a new path of opportunity. In this lesson, we need to listen to our own advice! For our businesses to grow, we need to apply the same lessons. The skills are there, the training is absorbed, and the desire is alive. It's time for action!

In chapter 10 of this book, you looked at "The Change Chart." The pivotal zone on the chart is the place where you make the choice either to return to the stages of fear, self-doubt, and loss of comfort, or find the courage to move to the stages of expectancy and courage which allow you to pursue real success. It's not enough to have the ability to coach; you also need to take bold steps to establish a successful coaching business.

THE BUSINESS OF COACHING

Starting your own business is one of the most powerful ways to take control of your life and fulfill your dreams—but doing it the right way is imperative if you want to avoid future regrets. These ten steps from the Small Business Administration can help you plan, prepare, and manage your business.

Step 1: Write a Business Plan

According to the Small Business Administration, the first step in starting a business is to write a business plan. This is a document that clearly establishes the objectives of a business, the strategy and tactics planned to achieve the objectives, and the expected profits, usually over a period of three to ten years. Banks require comprehensive business plans when new companies borrow money, but in your coaching business, the business plan is designed to help you clarify your direction, processes, resources, and expectations. A business plan includes several elements, beginning with an Executive Summary.

The executive summary is a snapshot of your business plan. It gives a quick glimpse of how your company is structured and your goals. The business plan lets investors and advisors see your company's potential, and therefore is the most important section of your plan. The executive summary appears first because it showcases the strengths of your overall plan. The components of an executive summary include:

- **The Mission Statement:** A brief statement that describes what your business is about.
- **Company Information:** Your business's formation, founders and roles, number of employees, and locations.
- **Growth Highlights:** Graphs and charts of the company's growth.
- **Your Products/Services:** Describe the products and services you provide as simply as possible. Be sure to include your areas of specialty (your niche if you have decided on one) such as Executive Coaching, Business Coaching, etc.
- **Financial Information:** Hourly rates, group rates, and other income must be clearly stated.
- **A Summary of Future Plans:** State the next steps for your business. Do you plan to bring in employees to assist with marketing, bookkeeping, partners to coach alongside you, etc.? Outline your plans for success and growth.
- **New and Start-up Business Plans:** Because you don't have as much information about your coaching business as an established company has, focus on your experience and background as well as training and the *why* behind starting your business.

Use market analysis information to persuade the reader how you will be successful in future plans.

Step 2: Get Business Assistance and Training

Take advantage of free training and counseling services available on the internet and locally from the SBA. Your local SCORE (www.score.org) and Small Business Administration (www.sba.gov) have a wealth of resources for you. If you're ready to begin the process, go to SCORE now.

Step 3: Choose a Business Location

Get advice on how to select a customer-friendly location and comply with zoning laws. In addition to meeting with clients in their offices or offsite, you can use Skype, Zoom, WhatsApp, Fuze, Google Hangout, ooVoo and other programs and applications to meet with clients online. A physical location isn't necessary for a start-up coaching business, but it may be an option later as your list of clients grows.

Step 4: Finance Your Business

Many new businesses fail because they are undercapitalized. Be financially prepared before you begin. As Steve Covey would say, "Begin with the end in mind." Construct a budget of anticipated expenses and revenues.

- Determine your take home pay, and then add all other expenses. You'll need this much in gross income to pay for your expenses.
- Divide the gross income by your hourly fee to come up with how many clients (at an average rate) you will need to support a profitable business.

Be sure to give estimates that are as close as possible to your realistic expectations. Since you aren't limited to an office to meet clients in person, the coaching profession has a very low financial start-up requirement. Video conferencing has made face-to-face coaching possible with clients all over the world. Barter is also a possibility. Consider offering coaching services in return for services others can provide for you. Example budget:

LINE ITEMS ANNUAL AMOUNTS

Estimated Take Home Pay	$60,000.00
Estimated Business Expenses (advertising, postage, office rental, auto expenses, etc.)	$10,000.00
Business Insurance (liability, errors and omissions insurance, etc.)	$5,000.00
Estimated Income Tax (local, state, federal)	$10,000.00
Estimated Social Security and Medicare.	$3,000.00
Estimated Health Insurance	$5,000.00
Estimated Retirement Investments	$6,000.00
Other	$1,000.00
TOTAL	**$100,000.00**

In this example, the new coach needs $100,000 in fees in order to generate a salary of $60,000.00. At a rate of $200 per hour, the coach will need to bill for five hundred hours a year to achieve this goal. Working fifty weeks a year, this coach must have ten billable hours of coaching per week.

Step 5: Determine the Legal Structure of Your Business

Decide which form of ownership is best for you: sole proprietorship, partnership, Limited Liability Company (LLC), C corporation, S corporation, nonprofit, or cooperative. Be sure to research the liability and tax implications of the business structure you consider. This is one of the most important decisions you will make for your coaching business. We recommend hiring an attorney and CPA to ensure you understand all the options, so you can make an informed decision.

Step 6: Register a Business Name ("Doing Business As")

Register your business name with both your local county government and state government, if applicable.

If you are ready to take this step, do so now.

Note: Many of the requirements for setting up a business listed are unique to each county, state, and country. It will be necessary to investigate and follow the regulatory directives for business start-ups in your own location. The following is an example (not an all-encompassing list) of the steps required to establish an S corporation in the state of Georgia, USA (whichever legal structure you select for your business will require a different set of criteria):

1) Determine the availability of the corporate name from the secretary of state's office by applying for "Name Reservation" that is effective for a thirty-day period.

2) Draft Articles of Incorporation and submit the completed articles with a "Transmittal Form" and filing fees to the secretary of state.

3) Once the Articles of Incorporation have been approved, it will be necessary to complete the (Federal) IRS Form 1023 "Election

by a Small Business Corporation" in order to receive approval from the IRS as an S corp.

4) Submit Form SS-4 to receive an Employee Identification Number (EIN).

5) Apply to the office of tax commissioner in the county in which your principal office is located for "Certificate of Occupancy" (Business License) and the payment of annual occupational taxes.

6) File the IRS Form 1120S and state form 600S each year.

This list may sound difficult; however, a CPA can walk you through these steps, and you will be set up to function as a business for years to come.

Step 7: Register for State and Local County Taxes

Register with your state to obtain a tax identification number, workers' compensation, unemployment and disability insurance. Contact the Internal Revenue Service (IRS) and your state's revenue agency to learn which tax identification number you'll need to obtain. As a sole proprietor, you may be able to use your Social Security number, unless you are using an assumed name. A CPA should be utilized to ensure that local, state, and federal laws are followed.

Your CPA will also give advice concerning tax requirements and the IRS code for periodic deposits. It's wise to make these deposits regularly throughout the year rather than wait until the end of the year to pay your taxes. If you are ready to take this step, do so now.

Step 8: Obtain Business Licenses, Permits, and Insurance

Get a list of federal, state, and local licenses and permits required for your business. Laws differ from state to state and even within a state. So, be sure to research the specific requirements (i.e. zoning/residential). Contact at least two competent business insurance agents to help you navigate your needs. Some products to consider include, but are not limited to:

- **Errors and Omissions Insurance** (or professional liability insurance)—This is a type of insurance for professionals (i.e., doctors, real estate licensees, consultants, and coaches). It protects from mistakes made in the course of work which unintentionally results in loss of life or money.

- **General Liability Insurance**—According to Oak Insurance of Naugatuck, Connecticut, "Liability insurance is a part of the general insurance system of risk financing to protect the purchaser (the "insured") from the risks of liabilities imposed by lawsuits and similar claims. It protects the insured in the event he or she is sued for claims that come within the coverage of the insurance policy. Originally, individual companies that faced a common peril formed a group and created a self-help fund out of which to pay compensation should any member incur loss (in other words, a mutual insurance arrangement). The modern system relies on dedicated carriers, usually for-profit, to offer protection against specified perils in consideration of a premium."

Step 9: Understand Employer Responsibilities

Learn the legal steps necessary to hire employees. Know the difference between an employee and an independent contractor, as defined by the IRS code (or regulatory system in your country), both for yourself and for those that work for you or do work on your behalf. This will save you a lot of money and prevent headaches.

If you are an independent contractor, you are self-employed. To find out what your tax obligations are, visit the Self-Employed Tax Center.

You are not an independent contractor if you perform services that can be controlled by an employer (what will be done and how it will be done). This applies even if you are given freedom of action. What matters is that the employer has the legal right to control the details of how the services are performed.

If an employer-employee relationship exists (regardless of what the relationship is called), you are not an independent contractor, and your earnings are generally not subject to self-employment tax.

However, your earnings as an employee may be subject to FICA (Social Security tax and Medicare) and income tax withholding. A CPA or accounting professional should be able to guide you in these matters.

Step 10: Find Local Assistance

Contact your local Small Business Administration office to learn more about how SBA can help.

CHAPTER 33

ACQUIRING CLIENTS

An effective marketing strategy is essential to expand your business. If you try to appeal to everyone, you'll appeal to no one. When you identify the people you want to work with and market your website to meet their needs, you've taken the first step in building the relationship. The specifics of your marketing content will answer the preliminary questions of those who might choose you as their coach. If you can demonstrate your specific interest in them and your experience in helping others with similar goals, they're far more likely to make the connection with you. Remember: Few people want coaches who are generalists; most want coaches who are experts who can address their particular needs.

The more knowledgeable you are in a specific specialty—the particular challenges and the solutions of your niche audience—you can focus your marketing efforts and achieve better results. As you become established in a niche, you will get more referrals and more clients.

The vast amount of niche coaching literature confirms that many coaches are more successful when they focus their marketing efforts on a particular set of clients or choose the right niche (their passion, expertise, and experience). It is logical, then, to assume that as the profession of coaching grows, it will be even more important to have a niche.

A coaching practice requires us to develop a mind for business, marketing, delegation, systems, and networking. Marketing is a vital element to establish a coaching presence in the community, and perhaps, around the world. Marketing is a strategic and focused positioning of a personal coaching brand, personality, and coaching products. Whether you are promoting your services as an individual or as a practice, you need to develop and implement a Coaching Marketing Strategy. In this chapter, each element will provide tools to assist you in marketing your practice.

One of the biggest challenges of marketing your coaching business is the fact that you are actually marketing yourself. You may be confident in your training and skill, but you might be hesitant to promote yourself. Marketing your own business allows you to control how you're perceived professionally and personally. Consider writing and publishing an online newsletter, writing a book or a blog, speaking at local service clubs, speaking at conferences, attending workshops, and other creative ways to become known.

Perhaps the most frequent question we hear is: "How do I get coaching clients?" The short answer is, "Market to whom you know." The next question is, "How?" Identify your target audience and how they will be drawn to you. The first factor is: "How do others know

I'm a coach?" The second important factor is, "Who is my audience, and where do they work, play, live, or worship?" These two factors are crucial to marketing, managing, and maintaining a coaching practice. But sometimes visibility isn't enough.

Coaching offers a vast array of possibilities for clients. It is a unique and personal process, whether you are coaching an individual or corporation. Carefully consider your answer to these questions: "What is the pain point that people will pay me to help them overcome?" or "What is the unrecognizable gap that coaching can resolve?" Determine their most pressing problems and fears. This will allow you to create quality content your prospects will happily devour, leaving them hungry for more.

To attract clients:

- Build a Database. Managing a database takes work. It's important to build a list of names and capture accurate contact information about existing and future clients.

- Create Webinars. Your coaching business is all about building a relationship of trust with your audience. Webinars can shorten the time to build this trust to as little as an hour.

- Ask Your Clients for Referrals. Asking, "Whom do you know that might benefit from my services?" is a simple, yet powerful way to meet new prospects. Let your clients know you are expanding your practice, and ask them if they know of anyone to whom you could offer a sample session.

- Form "Combo" Alliances. Form an alliance with suppliers, colleagues, or even your competitors to offer a "combo" package. For example: A life coach might form an alliance with a gym or weight-loss or stop-smoking program.

■ Pay Per Click Advertising. Pay per click (PPC) is a quick way to send people to your website. You might consider Facebook ads, Google AdWords, and LinkedIn ads. Platforms like Facebook make it simple to target members of your audience, making it easy to connect with your ideal clients through demographic, interest, and behavior-based advertising. Remember to allocate a budget for the PPC costs.

Create Referral Partnerships

Richard Fettke, in his Fettke.com article "50 Great Marketing Ideas for Coaches" also advocates, "Find out who may be able to refer their clients, friends, or contacts to you. Look for people you believe in, so that you can do the same for them. For example, an accountant may refer a new business owner to you to help her stay focused and on track as she grows her business. You may refer one of your clients to the accountant, so they can more wisely manage their money."

No business can be successful in a silo, so creating a community of support and advocacy in your industry and target market can be a huge benefit. Ironically, coaching can be an isolating role, especially if the primary coaching connections occur virtually instead of in person. To continue to grow personally and professionally, join coaching and business networking groups for support, encouragement, and accountability. Your competitors don't have to be your enemies. In fact, some of them can become your greatest supporters. And in fact, you may find that some people you don't enjoy coaching fit better with another coach, and another person's client may work better with you. In this way, you have potential to create a win-win situation.

Consider joining these networks:

- **International Coaching Federation (ICF)**—The ICF is the primary worldwide resource for business and personal coaches, and Fettke believes it's an important resource "for those who are seeking a coach. The ICF is an individual membership organization formed by professionals worldwide who practice and/or teach business and personal coaching. The ICF provides many resources and can help you meet other coaches, prospects, and leaders. The ICF also holds an annual conference where you can learn new marketing skills and tools." Look online to find a local or regional ICF chapter.

- **Chamber of Commerce**—Joining a local Chamber of Commerce can be a valuable source of leads and contacts with referral partners. You may also be able to write articles for their newsletters and give workshops to fellow members on your area of expertise.

- The **Association of Change Management Professionals (ACMP)** is a nonprofit professional association dedicated to advancing the discipline of change management. Change management is the practice of applying a structured approach to transition an organization from a current state to a future state to achieve expected benefits. Go online for more information about ACMP.

- The **Organization Development Network** focuses on developing organization capability through alignment of strategy, structure, management processes, people, and rewards and metrics. The ODN website provides insights and suggestions.

- The **Society for Human Resource Management (SHRM)** is the world's largest HR professional society, representing 285,000 members in more than 165 countries. This is a great resource to network with HR managers for internal, external, and executive coaching opportunities.

COACHING LEADERS

DR. DON BRAWLEY III
*Founder/CEO Influencers Global; Master Coach
Trainer, Dream Releaser Coaching*

Organizational leaders across industries, from C-suite to middle-management, embrace the benefits found in having a coach. Often these leaders retain a coach when their organization is going through a change, they have taken on a new role, or they have identified an area they would like to develop. It has long been theorized that the best ROI for leadership development comes from permanent behavior change. As a C-suite coach, I lead executives through the coaching process by establishing trust, enabling leaders to shift their mindset, and thereby, ultimately change their thinking and behavior.

I have had the privilege to work with C-suite leaders and executives across industries including multiple Fortune 500 companies. Just like the best sports athletes utilize coaches to become even better players, C-suite executives retain coaches to continue their development to become better leaders.

As a C-suite and executive coach, *I'm more intimate than a mentor but not as personal as a therapist!*

Without fail, I can say the primary C-suite coaching need always involves a change in mindset. This is because behavior is only the fruit of a root beneath the surface, and the root of every action is a mindset. When I say mindset, I mean the unseen beliefs, attitudes, and values that result in observable behavior. Change that brings even better business results is only realized through a sustained change in mindset.

For example, a leader may need to shift his mindset from *doing* the work that he has done so well to *delegating* it by empowering others. This can be difficult because doing the work is often what made the executive successful at climbing the organizational ladder in the first place, but it can limit him from being successful as a leader. In this case, the executive's mindset must shift from believing success and significance is found in actually doing the work himself to empowering others to get it done, even if they fail along the way.

Executives always come with a desire for growth that requires a shift in their mindset, and growth *always* requires change. Lasting change begins with mindset, not behavior. Regardless of why the executive is receiving coaching, I come alongside to help him experience a shift in his mindset that, in turn, will give him the personal and business results he desires. Change often isn't easy, but it is possible. Together, we define his desired result, create a pathway toward it, and measure progress, all the while enabling his personal growth. This all begins during our first session with a process called *contracting*.

Contracting is the process of defining the relational container that will hold the coaching relationship together. It is so essential to the coaching process that it's included in the ICF's eleven core competencies. Contracting may be written and formal, or verbal and informal. During the contracting process the coach and client align around what will happen and how it happens within the coaching context with the goal of the contract process being to establish trust.

During contracting, I align with my clients regarding what I expect of them during the coaching process and what they should expect from me. We clarify exactly what a coach does, discuss the responsibilities of a client, identify any previous experience working with a professional coach, and distinguish how the coaching process differs from consulting. When I consult, which is typically done in faith-based contexts and nonprofits, *I advise* my clients on the best approach forward. When I'm consulting in the faith-based world, I typically blend coaching with my consultation of senior leaders.

However, in C-suite coaching, I do not consult; rather, I use an inquiry-based coaching methodology to help my client clarify what she wants most and chart a pathway forward to attaining it. In this way, the client owns her decisions and unleashes the intrinsic motivation needed to accomplish her goals.

Also, during contracting, mutual confidentiality is explained. C-suite engagements may include a wide range of other stakeholders: the client, the client's manager, the client's peers, human resources, the coaching organization, the coach, the coach's supervisor, etc. In order for the client to feel safe enough to fully commit to the coaching process, confidentiality must be explicitly discussed, agreed upon, and honored throughout the engagement.

Further, we agree on logistics regarding the frequency of our meeting, scheduling, cancellations, missed sessions, and "stretch assignments" that are completed between meetings. Proper contracting enables alignment around mutual expectations, agreed upon boundaries, and desired results.

During contracting, I determine which of the four faces of coaching will best serve my client. For instance, while I never wear my consulting hat to a coaching engagement, some clients ask for my advice. They want to know my opinion from a leadership point of view and hear about other clients, who remain completely anonymous, to see how they handled similar circumstances. These clients want to see my *expert face*.

Other leaders, however, thrive in a dynamic that allows them to step back and get to the root of their challenge while coming up with their own solutions. I show up for these clients using my *counselor's face*, evoking deeper reflection and emotion while guiding them to see an old problem in a new way. Other leaders simply need to feel someone truly believes in them and sees that they still have untapped potential. For them I show up with my *supporter face*.

Still, others excel when they are challenged to attempt something radical and dream something even bigger. These clients appreciate very direct feedback. Perhaps this is because, more often than not, the higher a leader goes up the organizational ladder, the less honest people are with them. This dynamic can create blind spots for the leader. With these clients, I show up with my *challenger face*. I am more direct, challenging the client to uncover what she's been missing, and I do just a bit more telling than I would during a typical coaching session.

Regardless of the C-suite client's reason for coaching, I ensure trust is established from our first session, confidentiality is always honored throughout the journey, and I flex my style so that I show up regularly in ways that are in the best service of my client.

ACKNOWLEDGMENTS

Each time I hear a testimonial from a Dream Releaser Coaching (DRC) trainee about how their life has been "transformed" by going through the program, I am humbled and filled with gratitude for the dedication of the DRC team. DRC has an incredible team of trainers that have given their wholehearted effort to the coach training process. They have turned my dreams about developing Life Coaches into reality. The majority of our current team has been with DRC since its inception in 2010. I offer my heartfelt thanks to: Moren Adenubi, Jim Bolin, Paula Pérez Bonilla, Chris Bowen, Terry Bradley, Don Brawley, Mona Brawley, Robin LaGrow Buttler, Larry Carnes, Debbie Chand, Sam Chand, Maury Davis, William Flippin, Sherry Gaither, Craig Johnson, Danny Keaton, Mary Keaton, Betty Glover Palmer, Ofir Peña, Efrain De La Paz, Karen Robertson, Alice Rodriquez, Tony Rodriquez, Kim Schofield, and Jeff Smith.

Further, I offer my gratitude to each contributor to this work: Moren Adenubi, Chris Bowen, Don Brawley, Maury Davis, Teresita Glasgow, Nicholas John, Mike Kai, Karen Robertson, and Jeff Smith.

I am especially grateful to Lyn Eichmann, Director of Training, and Joseph Umidi, President of Lifeforming Leadership Coaching, for their invaluable assistance in our humble beginnings.

A very special note of thanks goes to writing maven, Patrick "Pat" Springle. For years, he has managed to take my very raw materials (notes, interviews, and ramblings) and make them into something harmonious. With his vast knowledge and writing proficiency, he can transform seemingly jumbled, disjointed, and incompatible concepts into a cohesive book like the one you are now reading!

One of my deepest core values is family. In our home, when one of us has a large project, we all have a large project. Everyone pitches in in one way or the other—from picking up the slack to editing to just in general lending a hand. This project was no exception. Thank you, Debbie, for taking care of a multitude of details for me. Rachel, your editing skills saved me so much time and effort, thank you. Zack was the lucky one this time—on active military duty elsewhere. Of course, my granddaughters, Adeline and Rose, are always the wind beneath my wings. And my husband, Sam, thank you for always being supportive of my dreams and believing in me this past half century. Of course, as you often say, my dreams are always expensive. You've been the best sponsor ever!

ABOUT THE AUTHOR: BRENDA C. CHAND

For Brenda Chand, 1975 was a pivotal year in her life, when she chose to devote her life to serving others. Even then, at the age of eighteen, her love for people in all walks of life motivated her to prepare academically. Her concentration of studies in formal education is testimony of her desire to serve.

She received a Bachelor of Arts in Biblical Education from Beulah Heights University (BHU) in 1977 with honors. In 2002, she received a Master of Ministry degree in Leadership from Southwestern Christian University. In 2012, she received the Doctor of Ministry degree from Oral Roberts University in Pastoral Care and Counseling.

In 1979, she was married to Samuel Chand. Their ministry led them to Portland, Oregon; Hartford, Michigan; and back to Atlanta, Georgia; in 1989 where Sam served as president of BHU (1989-2003).

Brenda served as adjunct instructor at her alma mater BHU from 2002 through 2013 in the area of leadership. She has taught such courses as: Spiritual Formation, Laws of Leadership, Leadership Coaching, Oral Communication, and Marriage and Family.

Brenda's role in ministry has been to be, first, a support for what God is doing through her husband. While pastoring, Brenda's ministry was flavored with diversity ranging from teaching nursery-age children to leading women's ministries to working with teens and the elderly. In addition, she has been a seminar and retreat speaker and is a contributing author in the book *Failure: The Womb of Success*. Most recently, she has written curriculum for Dream Releaser Coaching.

She is cofounder of Dream Releaser Coaching (accredited by the International Coaching Federation) where she holds credentials as Certified Leadership and Life Coach as well as Coach Trainer.

Her ministry areas include serving at home and abroad. At her home church, Brenda has been active in ministry. She has served as Assistant Pastor, Director of Women's Ministries, Teacher, and Leadership Development Coordinator. Brenda was one of the founders of The Rev. B. M. Chand School of Theology and Leadership in Lucknow, India, where she serves as Senior Advisor.

She is most passionate about teaching spiritual formation and developing others through life coaching.

She shares her love and life with her husband, Sam, two daughters—Rachel and her husband, Zack, and Debbie—and two granddaughters, Adeline Joy and Rose Marie.

ABOUT THE DREAM RELEASER COACHING PROGRAM
DREAMRELEASER.COM

efore joining a coaching program, you'll want to know if it meets your needs, helps you succeed, and is accredited and recognized. Dream Releaser Coaching (DRC) takes your desire to help others and trains you to become a Professional Certified Life Coach. We are accredited with the **International Coaching Federation (ICF)** with the status of Approved Coach Specific Training Hours (ACSTH). ICF is the largest coaching group and accrediting agency in the world. Graduates from DRC are eligible to apply for credentials with ICF at the Associate Certified Coach (ACC) and Professional Certified Coach (PCC) levels.

DRC has several experienced Coach Trainers who are credentialed through the ICF. These trainers provide the required mentor coaching to become credentialed. They have obtained a credentialing status which qualifies them to prepare you for your credentialing application according to ICF requirements.

Following are the tracks provided by DRC as well as the title you will receive upon completion of each one. Note that tracks 1-4 are required to complete our program, while simultaneously fulfilling the required training hours to be eligible to apply for credentialing with ICF.

- Track 1: Coaching Essentials—Associate Coach
- Track 2: Whole Life Coaching—Associate Certified Coach
- Track 3: Coaching with Sam Chand—Professional Coach
- Track 4: Building your Coaching Business—Professional Certified Coach
- Track 5: Professional ICF Credentialing
- Track 6: Coaching Specialties Electives

WHAT DREAM RELEASER COACHING OFFERS IN EACH TRACK

ICF Accredited	Yes
Program Length	Every Track is 10 weeks
Time Commitment	4 hours weekly (average)
1 on 1 Mentoring	Yes
Virtual Class	Yes
Teleclasses	Yes
Live Coaching Practice	Yes
Course Feedback	Yes
Live and Recorded Webinars	Yes
PDF Downloads	Yes
Video Content	Yes
Lifetime Access to Resources	Yes

Learn How to Start Your Own Coaching Business	Yes
Learn How to Market Yourself	Yes
Private Facebook Group	Yes
Payment Plan Options	Yes

You'll be assigned a personal coach and peer(s), and you will meet with them each week via telephone or Zoom during each track. Appointments will be scheduled at convenient times for all participants. There is one online summit per track (dates will be published accordingly).

NEXT STEPS

- Next Steps are assignments given for each week.
- Next Steps must be completed after reading each lesson before the teleconference/video call with your assigned coach trainer.
- Completion of Next Steps is a requirement to participate in the Summit.
- A Summit will be held in a major US city or online during week 7 of the track.

OUTCOMES

- Each track will be reviewed in its entirety in week 10.
- A comprehensive evaluation will be conducted.
- Certification will be issued depending on satisfying track requirements.

FOLLOWING ARE THE SPECIFICS
OF EACH OF THE TRACKS:

Track 1: Coaching Essentials is designed to equip the coach trainee with essential knowledge and skills required for coaching.

Our objectives for the lessons in this track are to ensure that the coach trainee grows and develops personally and becomes equipped with the basic skills to coach others. In this track you will begin to coach and be coached. We want you to enjoy the journey!

Specific topics discussed in Coaching Essentials include: The Elements of Coaching, Building Hope—Changing Lives, Changing Lives through Coaching, Motivational Interviewing, Steps toward a Desired Destiny, and Forward-Focused Coaching, along with many subtopics and life-application exercises.

Track 2: Whole Life Coaching builds on the basic knowledge gained from the Coaching Essentials track while focusing on the life of the coach trainee. The premise of the track is that self-awareness is one key to "living life by design and not by default."

This track will focus on an in-depth look at the life of the coach trainee through a series of instruments and exercises. In turn, the coach trainee will develop the skills to lead others through the process.

Topics in this track include: Personality Types and Definitions, Self-Discovery, Discovering and Overcoming Barriers, Discovering and Developing Personal Core Values, Balanced Living, and Life by Design—Not Default.

Track 3: Coaching with Sam Chand features the personal teaching and coaching of our cofounder. After many years of coaching thousands of people, we have discovered some important principles and practices. Whatever your sphere of coaching may be, these concepts will equip you to help your clients reach their goals.

The topics in this track are personal to the founder. They are topics that, in his experience, every leader faces; therefore, every coach will find himself or herself faced with the challenge of coaching others through these issues.

The topics for this track include: Focus, Vision Casting, Communication, Decision-Making, Choosing the Team, Leadership Development, Change vs. Transition, Conflict, Organizational Congruence, Financial Management, Time Allocation, Control vs. Delegation, Execution, Future Thinking, and Legacy.

Track 4: Building Your Coaching Business gives an overview of the major steps required to set up a business. Using the guidelines given by the Small Business Administration, this track breaks down each step and provides exercises that can be used to establish your coaching business.

In Track 4, you'll learn how to launch, brand, and grow your coaching business. We'll give you insights and resources to help you understand "the business of the business." Today, at a faster rate than ever before, coaching delivery systems are adapting and shifting. This track will help you be prepared for all the changes. We want you to thrive in a successful business, and we're excited about the possibilities open to you. We believe you can do *good* while doing *well*!

The topics for this track include: Monetizing Your Product, Business Structure, Writing a Business Plan, Insurance Matters, Marketing, and Assessments.

By the end of Track 4 . . .

Those who complete tracks 1–4 will have:

1) Mastered the essentials of coaching
2) Processed the important elements of your life: past, present, and future
3) Unpacked the wide range of issues every coach encounters
4) Learned to launch, brand, and grow your coaching business

Track 5: Professional ICF Credentialing track will prepare the qualified candidate to apply for professional coaching certification with the ICF. It includes the ten hours of mentor coaching required in the ICF credentialing process.

This includes:

- Weekly teleconferences/video calls with a DRC and ICF Credentialed Coach Trainer
- Next Steps—weekly assignments
- Summit—held online—recommended but not required
- Coaching practice and feedback

In this track you will take steps to fulfill the ICF requirements for credentialing. You are making a decision to take what you've learned from DRC (or another approved program) to become a Professional ICF certified coach. In this track, you will learn ICF criteria, merge DRC (or another program) learning and move into the next chapter of your life—becoming a dually certified coach.

Track 5 is designed to equip you to complete all of the necessary steps in order to receive ICF credentials. This includes a thorough examination of ICF Core Competencies and Code of Ethics, audio coaching and a transcribed session, required hours of mentoring from an ICF credentialed coach, coaching practicums, and practical suggestions and instruction for taking ICF's Coach Knowledge Assessment (CKA).

Outcomes
- Completed audio coaching and transcribed session to submit with ICF application
- Thorough knowledge of ICF Core Competencies
- Thorough knowledge of ICF Code of Ethics
- Preparation to take the CKA
- Full preparation to begin the ICF credentialing process

Track 6: "Electives" allow coach trainees who have completed Tracks 1-4 to be trained in specific areas.

The track includes:
- Your choice of 4 electives
- Completion of 2 lessons per elective
- Coaching sessions with coach trainers
- Next Steps—weekly assignments
- Summit—held online—not required

You may select any from the following list:
- Coaching Healthy Pastoral Teams
- The Challenge of Losing Weight

- Building Confidence
- Essential Components of Success
- Thriving Through Difficult Relationships
- Living Life on Purpose
- Business & Coaching Models
- Financial Freedom
- Strategic Change: Your Next Big Move

Our talents, experiences, interests, and passions enable us to become experts in specific areas. At Dream Releaser Coaching, we not only *recognize* your unique contributions—we *celebrate* them! The electives are offered to inform you, inspire you, and equip you to be the best coach you can be.

RESOURCES

UNSTUCK is a workshop that can be conducted in 1 ½ to 3 hours depending on the time allotted by one of our DRC staff!

WHAT'S SHAKIN' YOUR LADDER?
15 Challenges all Leaders Face by Sam Chand

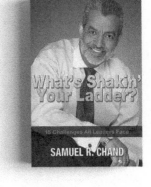

BIGGER FASTER LEADERSHIP: *Lessons from the Builders of the Panama Canal* by Sam Chand

To learn more visit
DreamReleaser.com

ADDITIONAL READING

BOOKS

Bandura, Albert. *Self-Efficacy: The Exercise of Control.* New York: W. H. Freeman, 2002.

Brock, Vikki G. *Sourcebook of Coaching History.* 2nd ed. USA: www.coachinghistory.com, 2014.

Cockerham, Ginger. *Group Coaching: A Comprehensive Blueprint.* Bloomington, IN: iUniverse, 2011.

Coe, Cindy, Amy Zehnder, and Dennis C. Kinlaw. *Coaching for Commitment.* 3rd ed. San Francisco, CA: John Wiley & Sons/Pfeiffer, 2008.

Collins, Gary R. *Christian Coaching: Helping Others Turn Potential into Reality.* Colorado Springs, CO: NavPress, 2002.

Crane, Thomas G. *The Heart of Coaching: Using Transformational Coaching to Create a High-Performance Coaching Culture,* San Diego, CA: FTA Press, 2007.

DiClemente, Carlo C. *Addiction and Change*. New York: The Guilford Press, 2003.

Fisher Gary L., and Thomas C. Harrison. *Substance Abuse: Information for School Counselors, Social Workers, Therapists, and Counselors.* 3rd ed. Upper Saddle River, NJ: Pearson Education, 2005.

Fournies, Ferdinand F. *Coaching for Improved Work Performance*. USA: McGraw-Hill, 2000.

Gallwey, W. Timothy. *The Inner Game of Tennis: The Classic Guide to the Mental Side of Peak Performance*. New York, NY: Random House, 1974.

Goldsmith, Marshall. *Coaching for Leadership: How the World's Greatest Coaches Help Leaders Learn*. San Francisco, CA: Jossey-Bass/Pfeiffer, 2000.

Goulston, Mark. *Just Listen: Discover the Secret to Getting Through to Absolutely Anyone*. USA: AMACOM American Management Association, 2010.

Hargrove, Robert. *Masterful Coaching*. Rev. ed. San Francisco, CA: John Wiley & Sons, Inc., 2008.

Harkavy, Daniel. *Becoming A Coaching Leader: The Proven Strategy for Building Your Own Team of Champions*. Nashville, TN: Thomas Nelson, Inc. 2007.

Homan, Madeline, and Linda J. Miller. *Coaching in Organizations: Best Coaching Practices from the Ken Blanchard Companies*. Hoboken, NJ: John Wiley & Sons, 2008.

Hughes, Marcia, L., Bonita and James Bradford Terrell. *Emotional Intelligence in Action: Training and Coaching Activities for Leaders, Managers, and Teams*. 2nd ed. San Francisco, CA: Pfeiffer/Wiley, www.pfeiffer.com, 2012.

Hunt, James M., and Joseph R. Weintraub. *The Coaching Organization: A Strategy for Developing Leaders.* Thousand Oaks, CA: Sage Publications, Inc., 2007.

Janis, Irving L., and Leon Mann. *Decision Making: A Psychological Analysis of Conflict, Choice, and Commitment.* New York: The Free Press, 1977.

Johnston, Ray. *The Hope Quotient: Measure It. Raise It. You'll Never Be the Same.* Nashville, TN: W. Publishing, an imprint of Thomas Nelson, 2014.

Logan, David, and John King. *The Coaching Revolution: How Visionary Managers are Using Coaching to Empower People and Unlock Their Full Potential.* Holbrook, MA: Adams Media Corporation, 2001.

Marquardt, Michael. *Leading with Questions: How Leaders Find the Right Solutions by Knowing What to Ask.* San Francisco, CA: John Wiley & Sons, Inc., 2005.

McLean, Pamela. *The Completely Revised Handbook of Coaching: A Developmental Approach.* San Francisco, CA: Jossey-Bass, 2012.

Miller, William R., and Stephen Rollnick. *Motivational Interviewing: Preparing People for Change.* 2nd ed. New York: The Guilford Press, 2002.

Morgan, Howard, and Marshall Goldsmith. *The Art and Practice of Leadership Coaching.* Hoboken, NJ: John Wiley & Sons, 2005.

Rogers, Jenny. *Coaching Skills: A Handbook*, 3rd ed. New York, NY: McGraw-Hill Education, 2012.

Scott, Susan. *Fierce Conversations: Achieving Success at Work and in Life, One Conversation at a Time.* New York, NY: Fierce, Inc., Berkley/Penguin Random House, 2017.

Snyder, C. R. *Handbook of Hope: Theory, Measures, and Applications*. San Diego, CA: Academic Press, 2000.

Stanley, Paul D., and J. Robert Clinton. *Connecting: The Mentoring Relationships You Need to Succeed in Life*. Colorado Springs, CO: Nav-Press, 1992.

Stolovitch, Harold D, Erica J. Keeps, with Marc J. Rosenberg. *Telling Ain't Training: Updated, Expanded, and Enhanced*. 2nd ed. Alexandria, VA: ASTD Press, 2011.

Stoltzfus, Tony. *Leadership Coaching: The Disciplines, Skills and Heart of a Christian Coach*. Charleston, SC: Book Surge Publishing, 2005.

Stoltzfus, Tony. *Coaching Questions: A Coach's Guide to Powerful Asking Skills*. USA: www.Coach22.com, 2008.

Umidi, Joseph. *Transformational Coaching*. Maitland, FL: Xulon, 2005.

Watzlawick, Paul, John H. Weakland, and Richard Fisch. *Change: Principles of Problem Formulation and Problem Resolution*. New York: W. W. Norton, 1974.

Webb, Keith E. *The Coach Model: For Christian Leaders*. Active Results, 2012.

Whitmore, John. *Coaching for Performance: Growing Human Potential and Purpose*. 4th ed. Boston: Nicholas Brealey, 2009.

OTHER

Clinton, J. Robert. "The Paradigm Shift: God's Breakthrough Processing that Opens New Leadership Vistas." Altadena, CA: Barnabas, 1993: 1-52.

Dream Releaser Coaching. https://www.dreamreleaser.com/.

International Coaching Federation. "ICF Code of Ethics." https://coachingfederation.org/ethics/code-of-ethics.

International Coaching Federation. "Credentials and Standards." https://coachingfederation.org/credentials-and-standards.

The A. A. Group. *Where It All Begins*. New York: The A. A. Grapevine, 2005.

INSPIRE

IMPACT CULTURE. INFLUENCE CHANGE

INTRODUCING THE INSPIRE COLLECTIVE

While many churches are effective in equipping Christians for ministry within their walls, some struggle to prepare them for service in other arenas—their workplace, their neighborhood, their social community.

But the call to be change-makers is for all believers: Artists, business people, civic servants, community leaders, educators, mechanics, stay-at-home parents, students, and wait-staff.

That's why the Inspire Collective was established, to help raise up true influencers who are kingdom-focused Monday through Saturday, not just on Sundays.

The Inspire Collective delivers a unique blend of inspiration and application, spiritual and practical, for those wanting to impact and influence their everyday world for Christ.

THE INSPIRE COLLECTIVE OFFERS

- MAGAZINE
- BOOKS
- STUDY RESOURCES
- COURSES
- LIVE CLASSES
- EVENTS
- LOCAL NETWORKS

FOUNDED BY
Mike Kai, Martijn van Tilborgh, Sam Chand